D0141893

SCRAPS of LIFE

SCRAPS of LIFE
Chilean Arpilleras

Chilean Women and the Pinochet Dictatorship

MARJORIE AGOSIN

Translated by Cola Franzen

THE RED SEA PRESS
Publishers & Distributors of Third World Books
556 Bellevue Avenue
Trenton, New Jersey 08618

Published in 1987/88
The Red Sea Press
556 Bellevue Avenue
Trenton, New Jersey 08618
U.S.A.

Copyright © 1987 Marjorie Agosin

All rights reserved. The use of any part of this publication, reproduced, transmitted in any form or by any means, electronic, mechanical, photocopy, recording or otherwise stored in a retrieval system without prior written consent of the publisher is an infringement of the copyright law.

Library of Congress Catalogue Card Number

Agosin, Marjorie
   Scraps of Life: The Chilean arpilleras:
   Chilean women and the Pinochet Dictatorship
   1. Politics/Women's Studies — Latin America
   I. Title
87-61508

   ISBN 0-932415-28-8 Cloth
   ISBN 0-932415-29-6 Pbk

Typesetting: On-Line Graphics
Printing: Hignell Printing Ltd.
Cover Photo: Emma Sepúlveda
Printed and bound in Canada.

CONTENTS

ACKNOWLEDGEMENTS

This book was not born of the imagination, but of the concrete experiences of the Chilean women who live in the poor neighbourhoods of Santiago de Chile. To them this book is dedicated. I offer them my grateful thanks for allowing me to use their voices to tell the story of their reality to the outside world.

Many people have helped me during the long periods of the gestation and elaboration of this work, product of almost eight years of study and reflection. My special thanks to Maria Eugenia Lira, director of the arpillera workshops sponsored by the Vicarate of Solidarity, and to Cola Franzen, not only for her sensitive translation, but for her collaboration and support throughout the writing of this book. I am also grateful to Wellesley College for granting me a year's leave so that I might have the time to write the book, and for their constant support of my work.

I offer special thanks to my editors, and Ann Wallace, Publisher, of Williams-Wallace, who offered me so much encouragement, and to Robert Molteno of Zed Press.

Finally, as always, I would like to thank my husband, John Wiggins, for his love and encouragement in this project; for the many times he accompanied me to meetings across the United States so that I might show the arpilleras and talk about the women who make them. Thanks to him, to the others mentioned here, and to many whose names I cannot record here for lack of space, the stories in this book have been revealed.

M.A.

THE ARPILLERISTA

The *arpillerista*,
artisan of remains
burns with rage and cold
as she tenderly
picks through the remnants of her dead,
salvages the shroud of her husband
the trousers left after the absences
submerges herself in cloth of foaming, silent blood
and though she is fragile she grows large,
sovereign over her adobe hut,
her ragged scraps
and determined to tell her story
truer than the tale woven by her
sister Philomena.

Disruptive and beautiful she
puts together her flayed remnants
like a greenish and forgotten skin
and with her disguised thimble
hidden in the pocket of her modest apron
and her harmless needle
she conjures up victorious armies
embroiders humble people smiling, become triumphant
brings the dead back to life
fabricates water, bell towers, schools, dining rooms
giant suns
and the Cordillera of the Andes
peaks opening like portals
of this splendid city.

— *Marjorie Agosin*

TESTIMONY

I am very pleased that Marjorie Agosin has written a book about her experiences under a dictatorship, as well as the experiences of other Chilean women. Ms. Agosin is a sensitive and dedicated Chilean who has been able to pick up the subtle darkness of a dictatorial regime, which is just as brutal in many ways as the out-and-out torture and imprisonment. Old friends turn their backs on you. Distrust and suspicion develop in human relations. Fear guides all one's actions. This breaking down of the fabric that holds the society together is part of the deliberate design of the wielders of power and is a tool used to maintain power.

Ms. Agosin writes eloquently and beautifully of her native land and describes its anguish and pain. She tells the stories of brave and heroic women who have not only survived under the dictatorships in Latin America, but have emerged from these political disasters as leaders for decency, human rights, and for the building of a world where children can feel secure and free from brutality and torture.

We must all be concerned about this backlash on the road to a just society, the uprooting of democratic institutions, replacing them with the evils of barbarism and totalitarianism.

This book is a testimony to what is the worst in human functioning and what is the best in the spirit and soul of humankind.

Margarita Papandreou

PROLOGUE

In 1970 my native Chile was converted into a divided country, infected by fear and suspicion. Social and political groups that had lived together in relative harmony suddenly became fierce and violent antagonists. People around me began to distrust not just others but also themselves. A newly-elected government, populist and socialist, awoke fear and misgiving among those not yet prepared for the political and social readjustments that would address the claims of the most oppressed groups of the population. But during the years from 1970 to 1973 it was still possible to speak, criticize, discuss, read opposition newspapers, or just listen. Chile was still a free country. We were not yet afraid of silence.

After the military coup occurred on September 11, 1973, Chile was a severed country, a prison where people considered "bad", who were often the young or poor, students, intellectuals, artists and writers, were imprisoned, tortured, and murdered, —labelled "disappeared" — by those who had seized the country. A state of terror was imposed on the entire population. Everybody in Chile was afraid during the first days of the coup. Nobody knew what was going to happen, and even the credulous women who had given their jewels to help the cause of the Fatherland—to help the opposition forces that initiated the coup — were also afraid when bullets started zinging through their peaceful homes in the elegant quarters of the city.

But beyond political analysis, statistics, and history — arbitrary and never objective — I intend to tell as simply as I can how a group of Chilean women surmounted fear, how they found the audacity, the courage, to leave their homes and search for their missing loved ones in the claws of the dictatorship. I want to tell their words and their thoughts, to report on how they got together and what they expect to accomplish through their actions. Above all, I want to explore the rise of a collective voice and the collective action that has occurred in the chronicles of the arpilleristas of Santiago: "Here the guilty will have to be judged, and judged without amnesty, so that those responsible will be punished, and none of this that has happened will happen again. This will have to occur when democracy is restored, when we return to being a free country as we were years ago. As for me, I would like to see a government without killing, without torture, without massacres, and let it be a country of brothers."[1]

During the years between 1980 and 1985 I kept returning to Chile, always feeling a deep fear, because the more I learned about what the military could do, *with absolute impunity*, the more terrified I became. Finally, I saw this was precisely what they wanted: to terrify and paralyze the people into passivity, and I decided then I would not let them intimidate me. I chose not to be afraid of fear.

With the aid of the Vicarate of Solidarity (an organization of the Catholic Church concerned especially with human rights, that operates under the aegis of the office of the Archbishop of Santiago; see details Chapter III), I visited, during those five years, many workshops of the arpilleristas, the women who make the small appliquéd and embroidered wall hangings called *arpilleras* that show scenes from their daily life. The women make the arpilleras to earn extra money for basic necessities. I became especially close with the arpilleristas who were also members of the Association of Families of the Detained-Disappeared, each one having a family member who was missing. I identified with this group of women in a special way: I learned to listen to them, even though at that time I thought that listening did not mean acting. But by listening to them I have succeeded in writing their story. However, there are many things from our time together that I have forgotten, details that have slipped my mind. I mostly just stayed by their side as they went about their regular chores. I preferred not to use the paraphenalia of journalists and interviewers, tape recorders and so on. I did not want to inhibit them and I expecially did not want to compromise their already precarious position by recording their free and frank conversation. It was a strange time for me in the land of the arpilleristas: sometimes waiting for hours until it was possible for us to meet; the interminable bus rides, sometimes involving five changes before I could reach the outlying shantytowns, poor and under siege, where many of the women lived.

I felt in my heart that the story of these Chilean women had to be told. The arpilleras have travelled far and wide in countries of the west by now, and have been widely written about in newspapers and magazines. But I wanted to talk about the individual women who make them, and the group they have become. How did it happen? How did they manage to do it?

I am neither historian nor political scientist; I am a poet. My study does not pretend to offer explications for the causes of the repression in Chile, or the economic crisis that consumes the country, nor will I attempt to give an accurate body count of the tortured and the disappeared. No, that is not my intention nor does it lie within my abilities. There are others better able to write of those matters.

My greatest hope is that someone reading these pages in the future will be inspired to think about other brave and heroic groups of women who have emerged from the political disasters of Latin America — women such as the Mothers of the Plaza de Mayo in Buenos Aires, the Group of Mothers of El Salvador and the Group of Mutual Support (called GAM in Spanish) in Guatemala. It is important to examine how women have managed to survive under drastic dictatorship — how they kept going; how they stayed whole and human. We need to know of their failures and successes, what lessons from the past had an impact on their daily life and their public life.

I am profoundly grateful to the Chilean arpilleristas who taught me the value of life, the value of left-over scraps; who taught me persistence and a true desire of justice for all. From these women I learned to listen and then to tell, and in spite of all the adversities, I learned to hope for a more just and human society. It is to these women that I dedicate this book, as well as to my mother who taught me that even though I had bread and a roof over my head I must never forget those who don't.

FOOTNOTE

1 Testimony of the mother of a disappeared one from Patricia Politzer, *El miedo en Chile* (Fear in Chile). Santiago: Ediciones Chile y América, 1984.

CHAPTER 1

EMERGING FROM THE SHADOWS: WOMEN OF CHILE

Approaching the land of my childhood, familiar sights, sounds and smells fill my eyes and ears: the forests, the Pacific, restless and blue, the special smells of Santiago, the dusty cardboard huts, my grandmother's face, growing ever more transparent but also more tender. The faces of dead friends flash before my eyes; they sleep peacefully now, no longer caught in the immense agony of this remote country squeezed between the Cordillera of the Andes and the sea. I have come back to an imprisoned country to find a policeman with an attack dog on every street corner, supposedly to "insure the order of the nation." Chile, the country that was an example of democracy in Latin America, a tiny territory of the continent that elected a Marxist as president, Salvador Allende in 1971, now victim of one of the most violent dictatorships existing in the world today.

Slowly I descend the steps of the plane. It is a radiant day, dry with the special Andean sun that makes the air smell of ripe peaches. It is all so familiar to me and at the same time so strange. The moment the plane lands is the most terrifying for the traveller who returns, especially for the native-born Chilean, since one can never know whether entry will be denied or allowed. The international police do not find my name on the list of those deemed "dangerous for the security of the nation." Yes, you may enter. I leave trembling with relief.

So I enter my country that is now not mine, that belongs to

1

nobody except to those in uniforms who have taken over every street corner and who use their constant vigils as one more weapon to prevent us from thinking, living, being.

Evening on the Chilean coast: a mackerel sky criss-crossed with clouds that resemble free-running fish on their way to infinity. I begin to re-acquaint myself with my past and my present self. I find a fearful abyss between my story and the stories of those who have continued to live in the country. I have never been imprisoned, have never been blindfolded, but today there are many thousands of Chilean citizens being blindfolded and imprisoned. I have never had a blindfold removed to watch the torture of someone dear. Many Chileans have. I was one who left Chile when it was still free, and now returns to try and renew the ties to the ephemeral time of childhood.

We go to my house, or to what I still think of as my house — it is my grandmother's house. I recognize the taste, the freshness of the air, the freshness of nights near the sea. It delights my shoulders, my skin. I wrap my old woollen shawl around me, the one that I always leave in my grandmother's house, for all my returns. She had remembered to bring it to the airport for me to wear home. We walk hurriedly and in silence, anxious to get home before one o'clock in the morning when the curfew begins. On top of all the other restrictions of our liberty, they have added the hated curfew. And nobody wants to be surprised and defenseless on the deserted streets by the policemen and their dogs.[1]

Once inside the familiar house, I approach the window timidly and look out. The city is absent, solitary. The new and sinister silence of the streets thunders in my ears. My city, my country, resembles a vast uninhabited plaza where street lamps no longer shine on lovers or brighten the way for energetic young people. The plaza is a ghostly skeleton, a hallucinating phantasmagory, empty of people, empty of animals. Only the benches remain and the sound of boots takes possession of our city and our dreams. From the window I see two homeless beggar women, putting their belongings into a rickety metal cart. Their cancerous black shawls around their shoulders, even these women are afraid, as I am. They leave to sleep

2

in some uncertain place this night, or perhaps they will be lucky enough to find refuge in some abandoned building.

In the morning light I greet my country with the same open-hearted innocence I felt when my childhood friends and I tumbled in the sand and believed we would all grow up to be queens, happy and free.

So I come back to Chile, although I have never really been away; even blindfolded I would recognize the way back to my house or the faces of schoolmates. But this time I have come for another purpose: to hear the stories of some remarkable women so that later I can re-tell them — the women who have emerged as the conscience of this benighted nation, the women who make up the membership of the Association of Families of the Detained-Disappeared.[2]

This organization, made up almost entirely of women, was formed in 1974 under the protective wing of the Vicarate of Solidarity of the Catholic Church, a body of the Church that is concerned with defending human rights and functions under the special protection of the Archbishop, now Cardinal, of Santiago.

How does it happen this group could organize in a country where essentially all organizations are forbidden? The answer bursts from the mouths of these unusual women. They tell me that after the overthrow of the Allende government in 1973, they began to see each other day after day at jails, courthouses, and tribunals because all of them were coming to inquire for family members who had disappeared, to ask if anyone knew of their whereabouts. Drawn together in their pain and despair they formed a group so that together they might find out the truth.

Perhaps the most diabolical invention of the Latin American dictatorships, practiced especially in Chile, and in Argentina until their recent return to democracy, is that of making people disappear. The term *disappearances* was used for the first time to describe a specific governmental practice which was applied on a wide scale in Guatemala after 1966, in Chile toward the end of 1973 and in Argentina beginning in March, 1976. *To disappear* means to be snatched off a street corner, or dragged from one's bed, or taken from a movie theatre or a café either by police, soldiers, or men in

3

civilian clothes, and from that moment on, to disappear from the face of the earth, leaving not a single trace. It means that all knowledge of the *disappeared* is totally lost. Absolutely nothing is to be known about them. What was their fate? If they are alive, where are they? What are they enduring?[3] If they are dead, where are their bones?

The details of the technique and practice of *disappearances* is now coming to light in Argentina. Immediately after the return to democracy, a commission headed by the novelist Ernesto Sábato was appointed by President Alfonsín to investigate the disappearances. After a two-year-long inquiry the commission issued a report which has now been published.[3a] As a result, the trials of some of those deemed responsible have taken place in Buenos Aires in a civilian court. Accused in the first trial were three generals, all former leaders of the Junta, three admirals and three brigadier generals. Sentences have been handed down (life imprisonment in some cases) and many more cases are being prepared for trial. Obviously this turn of events in a neighbouring country means that the Junta in Chile has become more entrenched, more ruthless and more desperate to remain in power.

We should also add here *the fact that people were disappearing* in Argentina was brought to public attention by the women who have become known as the Mothers of the Plaza de Mayo, who began to draw attention, especially in 1979, by marching in front of the Presidential Palace every Thursday at noon, wearing white kerchiefs on their heads, sometimes carrying lighted candles and always carrying photographs of their children or grandchildren who had disappeared. At first the government denied that anyone had disappeared, and called the women *Las Locas, the Madwomen*. The Madwomen are still there, and they say they will stay there until every *disappeared* has been accounted for and every responsible person brought to justice.

To return to Sábato's findings for a moment, it was discovered that most of the *disappeared* were tortured to death, or to near death, and then disposed of in the easiest way possible for the officials, either thrown into mass graves at night, (many of these mass graves have now been excavated in Argentina) or thrown from helicopters into the Rio de la Plata or other bodies of water. Some of the bodies recovered from the river showed death was by drowning, that is, the victims were still alive when thrown from the helicopters.

As though the horror suffered by the *disappeared* themselves were not enough, there is the other horror, that experienced by the families of the *disappeared*. Rosa tells me that existence after a family member has disappeared is the most terrible agony that can be imagined. She is unable to go on. Her voice breaks and she begins to cry. To live with the reality of a disappeared one is to live permanently with absence, with emptiness, with uncertainty, in limbo. It is, as Eloisa says, to knit socks while knowing the person they are intended for may never return. It is to know that "although they are not in the street, they are not in the neighbourhood, their presence is felt everywhere. It is in the things they touched, in the book they were reading that is still left open at the same page, waiting. The neighbours who knew them think, here is the house where they lived, and there is the corner where they were taken. Everybody knows they must be somewhere, perhaps alive or perhaps dead."[4]

The women of the Association of Families are ready to talk immediately; they need to talk, to make sure that their story, so tragic and so common, (indeed it is still a daily occurrence), be told, be known, inside as well as outside the country. We spend many hours together in a patio inside the offices of the Vicarate in Santiago. It seems to me that there at last we can breathe, we can dare to speak without worrying that we might be surrounded by spies and enemies. For a moment at least we do not feel afraid, but the dark happenings of which they speak continue to occur every day in broad daylight as well as in the dangerous dark. Every day in some corner of the planet someone is being tortured, someone disappears, and it happens not only in the Chile of Pinochet.[5]

Personal contact with the families of the detained-disappeared is a profoundly moving experience for both the families and for visitors. The Association itself has become a family, its members brought together by pain and loss; they cling to one another and find

5

consolation in their closeness. They tell me, this Association is the family we lost; this is our family now. It often happens that other relatives don't want to hear about the tragedy of a disappearance; they don't want to be involved, they prefer not to know about it. But with members of the Association, it is different. "If one of us is missing one day, the others will start asking about the missing one. We would want to know what has happened. And so we don't feel completely abandoned."[6] For the observer listening to them talk, the experience is so devastating that no one can be left untouched by it.

I remember one meeting with thirty women in December, 1984 was delayed for more than an hour because the women had an appointment with officials of the Department of Interior concerning the *disappeared*. As I waited I thought of their years, their decade and more of waiting, and I began to realize the dimensions of the uncertainty and anguish in which they lived.

When they came, they were of all ages, from 20 to 70. They seemed strong, confident, and walked with firm steps. We sat down in a circle; I asked them if the tape recorder bothered them. They all said no, that they wanted to give their full names and tell their stories in their own voices so that those outside would know what had happened to them. They began to talk, each one reliving exactly the date and place of the detention or the last moment when the disappeared one was seen. For some of them, that day in December happened to be a fateful anniversary since many of their *disappeared* were first detained on that same day in December, 1974, exactly eleven years before.

Their voices began to mingle and suddenly I saw how fragile they were, how tired, how exhausted by their constant peregrinations, their rituals of protest. When the voice of one ceased, another continued; with their stories they wove a strong cord that bound them together. At times the voices became jumbled, but the story was always the same: loneliness, abandon, absence, uncertainty, injustice.

However, what is so moving is their profound determination to find the truth, an almost impossible task in a country ruled by a stringent dictatorship. However, as part of their effort, the women organize various collective acts of protest that might be called ritualistic in nature, that have had a major impact on the political and social history of Chile and on the international movement for human rights.

Since 1978 these symbolic acts have taken place regularly in Santiago. Their essential purpose is to make public in a dramatic way the fact that citizens have disappeared and also to pay open homage to the *disappeared* themselves, to keep their memory alive. The Association's motto is: "For life or for peace, tell us where they are."

In 1979 the women carried out a long hunger strike in public view. Wearing photographs of their disappeared ones pinned to their clothing, they chained themselves to the fence surrounding the National Congress Building in downtown Santiago. The chains were a reminder of the pain caused by the absence of the loved one. By deliberately imprisoning themselves with chains the women could participate in the suffering of their disappeared ones. The photograph worn on the body was another way of feeling closer to the absent ones.

The women who took part in this ritual were arrested and imprisoned. The prison experience, which included being stripped naked and photographed as well as being humiliated in numerous other ways, only made them more determined and made them feel even more closely bound with the detained-disappeared. When the women were released from prison, other members of the Association met them to offer the keys of their chain locks with flowers attached to them symbolizing victory and hope.

This dramatic event occurred after another event had attracted large participation and attention: the pilgrimage to Lonquén, an abandoned mine not far from Santiago where a mass grave was discovered in November, 1978. To call attention to this macabre finding, a human chain was formed consisting of 1500 people that reached all the way from Santiago to the entrance of the mine. There were speeches at the mine, but no political slogans. It was the intention of the Association that the dead be publicly mourned and honoured and that the world know of the criminal act that had taken place there. In this manner the massacre of Lonquén was made known and one more step was taken toward discovering the truth.

Those who took part in the memorial at Lonquén say it should be made into a kind of sanctuary to ensure that such tragedies never again occur. "We should commit ourselves to make Lonquén a blessed spot. May it be a very revered spot, so that never again will a hostile hand be raised against any other person that lives on the earth."[7]

The Association's acts of public ritual take place on the sharp edge between life and death. The sequence of events that began with chaining themselves to the fence in front of the former National Congress, dissolved by the Junta, the arrests, the releases, being greeted by flowers by the other members, all symbolize a return from death and an affirmation of life. The desire to live, to make public homage to the *disappeared*, is the only motivation for their continued search.

These women affirm life in their public rituals dedicated to the *disappeared*. They speak often in their daily conversation about life in all its aspects — of giving life, the common and daily miracle of being alive. It is precisely this passion for life that provides them with the possibility of irradicating pain and death. There is a continuous affirmation of the value of the family and above all there is an insistent attention given to the disappeared one. They speak about their children, when they were little and went to school. One says, "I want to see my son running free across the sand when he returns." Together with the affirmation of life, the human body is a very important reference for these women. They often speak of physical pain, the wounds caused by the disappearances. It seems that wearing a photograph of the missing one attached to the clothing or in a locket around the neck is a way of feeling closer to them and provides some feeling of consolation. One mother talks about her constant search:

"Could anyone imagine what it is like to search for a loved one in a society said to be 'normal' but which is suddenly transformed for me into a fortress enclosed by great closed gates. And the people at the gates always answer in a bored, laconic way: "He couldn't have been detained. He is not in our Cardex file."[8]

Other collective rituals are performed regularly by the Association members in order to insure that the *disappeared* are not forgotten. As a group, the women of the Association seem untiring, invincible. But looking at the individual women, they seem exhausted, as if all of a sudden they had been swallowed up by the diabolical shadow world of governmental bureaucrats who pretend to know nothing, make no reply. The women often huddle silently inside the tangled whirlwind of their days and seem to contemplate the reality of their lives, the certainty of their deaths. Gone now the feverish hope of the early years, between 1973 and 1974, as the possibility of finding the disappeared ones alive fades and what is looked for now is proof of death, a burial place, and some transcendent meaning for this enormous tragedy.

Since the membership of the Association is made up almost entirely of women, it is worthwhile to speculate on the reasons why this is so. Some say it is because it is mostly men who have disappeared and the women are left to search for them. But there are many women in the Association who have husbands and say their husbands prefer not to become involved in Association activities for fear of looking ridiculous, chaining themselves to fences, carrying candles, and so forth. But in the end, the answer seems to be "there are certain things that men do not do," and we are face to face with the old attitude of machismo. The term "feminism" rarely entered into our conversations. The women do not see their actions as a form of liberation of their sex, and when they refer to "liberation", as they do quite often, they mean it in its widest sense; they mean the liberation of all people and human dignity for all.

The most crucial phenomenon that has occurred in women's lives during the eleven years of the Pinochet regime is the fact that they have been turned into civic guerrillas. They have abandoned their traditional roles of housewife or domestic servant and have gone out into the streets to protest. They fill the public spaces and were for years *the only visible force protesting vigorously against the Pinochet government*, and this has been true from the beginning of the Association. Just when it seemed there were no paths of protest possible against this dictatorship, the women appeared in the streets and plazas wearing their white kerchiefs. They left their kitchens with the ubiquitous stew pot on the stove, and began to march proud, courageous, unafraid. They tell me when they are beaten by police or interrogated about the whereabouts of their children, they never let the jailors see them cry.

The political implications of the actions of these women are so enormous that they themselves are unaware of the dimensions. The most obvious implication is they serve as an example of courage for other groups opposed to the regime. Nevertheless, one must make it very clear that these women, in their lives before Pinochet, did not participate in any political party. They were mothers similar to those in the Plaza de Mayo in Buenos Aires, they were wives, sisters, living traditional lives. The upheaval of their personal lives obliged them to take some action. Again, we observe that women are moved to political activity by problems of a personal nature, by personal concern for the family, by the maternal instinct to nurture and protect, at all costs. But in the case of the women in the Association, personal politics has been transformed into collective politics which in turn has come to express the conscience of a people. One woman says: "Because of all this suffering we are united. I do not ask justice for my child alone, or the other women just for their children. We are asking for justice for all. All of us are equal. If we find one disappeared one I will rejoice as much as if they had found mine."[9]

Drawing together, when faced with a crisis and creation of community networks, converts women into an extremely powerful political force in epochs of crisis. The process that occurred in Argentina with the Mothers of the Plaza de Mayo is now occurring in El Salvador, in Beirut, and in other countries.

Invariably the women of the Association are asked what will happen when they find out the answer about their loved ones: Will they go back to their homes the same as before? They answer with a resounding No! They begin talking about how much there is to do, of the enormous social changes the country must make. Then I understand that this new political eruption born of personal tragedy and sorrow will not be dissipated. It will continue burning within the hearts of each of these women, transformed now into women warriors for peace, for justice, and for truth.

When our meetings ended I was devastated just from hearing their stories. Now I felt one of them; I was no longer an impartial observer. I could see in my mind's eye Anita or Elaida, frail but determined, going day after day from one prison to another, making the rounds of the detention centres, enduring long hunger strikes. Here they are next to me, sometimes trembling and sometimes laughing, so fragile in their innocence and searching. Then all of a sudden it seemed as if I was speaking with giants. They embraced me, and this great strength of theirs, together with their constant sadness, remains engraved in my memory and in my heart. Some of them give me the small snapshot of their disappeared one that they wear around their necks to show to the outside world; others ask me to tell their stories on every street corner. I can only write about them, and hope to arouse the conscience of a few people who may read these words. Writing is my only weapon, my only way of fighting with them, and I make a vow never to desert them, never to fall into the evil of silence.

The Arpilleristas

Latin America is a country of artisans, as Pablo Neruda said so many times. The markets of Latin America display a range of vibrant colours of weavings and embroideries, wooden objects, clay vessels, small statues, all worked patiently by the hands of humble and often forgotten artisans. Women work their magic to create stories with bits of cloth, needle and thread. In Chile today, the typically feminine crafts of sewing and embroidering have become a way of denouncing the oppressive government of Pinochet. The tender and delicate needlework of years ago has now been turned into a powerful weapon against the enemy. This is the case of the Chilean arpilleras, small wall hangings with figures superimposed on the cloth to create scenes full of vitality and movement, whose principal effect is that of political denunciation.[10] *Arpillera* means burlap in Spanish and since the backing cloth is often of burlap or other feed or grain sacks, the finished work has come to be called *arpillera*.

The group of women that began making arpilleras in 1974 were also members of the Association of Families of Detained-Disappeared. The Vicarate of Solidarity sponsors the arpillera workshops, buys the finished work from the women and sends it abroad to be sold. The arpilleras are not allowed to be shown or sold in Chile. The trafficking of arpilleras is essentially clandestine, but it continues to grow in spite of the government's efforts to stop it. The Vicarate also provides legal help for women of the workshops in their search for the *disappeared*.

Irma, who has now been a member of the arpillera group for more than eleven years says they began to make arpilleras as a way of earning money to help buy food for their families, and that their intentions were not so much to denounce as simply to show what had happened to them, their families and the country. The result was the same. These simple cloth pictures of arrests, beatings, bodies being buried in haste at night, empty pots, empty chairs are a devastating indictment of the Junta's policies. Once again we see how personal tragedy led to group activity and consciousness.

Each arpillera is a small scene from the life of the woman who creates it; just as their lives have been torn into pieces, the arpillera also consists of scraps of left-over material, put together slowly and in sorrow. Mireya says it took her many months to make her first arpillera that showed the detention of her son, but she did it finally, thanks to the support of her friends in the group. They say the arpillera workshop is their life, their daily bread, also a way of feeling accompanied in their sadness. The arpillera is not a creative competition but a way of sharing the preoccupations and worries of their everyday lives.

Just as the protest activities of the Association have had a major impact on the civic conscience inside Chile, the arpilleras have made their major impact outside the country, for reasons mentioned earlier. The interest in them has become so great that there are now thirty-one workshops, most of them located in the poorer neighbourhoods of Santiago. The money earned is fairly significant for jobless women, but perhaps of more importance is the sense of dignity that comes from working.

Once again we are together in a patio of the Vicarate. It is summer in Chile and the splendid, generous sun seems to erase at least momentarily the conditions of terror and despair in which these women live. I see them "sacando sus trapitos al sol", bringing their bits and pieces out into the sun, a phrase that in its figurative meaning in Chile means to get to the bottom of something, to learn the truth. As a writer might put words together, they put their scraps together with concentration and loving care. They sometimes stop to look at each other's work and to comment on it. At times the silence weighs down as when Irma finished her arpillera and we sat wordless as she relived the event she just pictured: the arrest of her son and daughter-in-law on a downtown street in Santiago by three men dressed completely in black and carrying submachine guns. The arpillera gives a more powerful account of that moment than any book or newspaper story ever could. I think to myself, what courage, what strong weapons are hidden in Irma's fingers.

Sitting next to Irma is Mercedes who finds it very difficult to talk. She become despairing as she tries to tell me the meaning of her arpillera and manages finally to tell me it shows how alone she feels. There is only a table and an empty chair, but in a little pocket sewn on the back, she has placed a piece of paper with the following message:

This arpillera represents the detention of my son who has been a detained-disappeared for ten years now. There has been no response. Help me to find him since the years are now weighing me down. I am a mother and a widow in a calamitous situation. The only favour I ask of God and the Virgin is that strength and courage be granted me to keep going until I find my son. Thank you.

Then comes Ana, the director of the group. Her arpillera has a photograph of her disappeared brother and an embroidered slogan that says:

TRUTH AND JUSTICE FOR THE DETAINED-DISAPPEARED

Another arpillera is just completed before my eyes. It bears a simple and eloquent message:

CAIN, WHERE IS THY BROTHER?

These arpilleras of brightly coloured scraps speak of pain and also of hope. With their big round suns and the peaks of the Andes framing the background, these simple cloth pictures assembled by women, some illiterate, some from the upper levels of society, travel to the far corners of the earth speaking for those who have no voice. Each arpillera completed and sent outside the country is another link between the oppressed people of Chile and the free outside world. The women who make them use their pain to try to forge a just society for all. That is the message to the rest of the world from these women warriors for peace.

The women who belong to the Association of Families of the Detained-Disappeared and the women of the arpillera workshops do not belong to any particular political party; they are not interested in gaining traditional political power. What they are working for is to form an alliance that would reach across all party and class lines and would be dedicated to the liberation of a people, a country. This is the feminine form of political action where personal power is not the goal, but collective power is sought because it is perceived as the only instrument of change.

It is impressive to see women from all economic strata working together against the dictatorship of Pinochet. They have already won in the sense that they have shown they are not afraid to stand up against his tyranny. These women are the main source of public opposition to the dictatorship. What they do has international significance. The actions taken alone might not seem terribly important, but they add up: women at the prisons waving their white handkerchiefs so the prisoners will know they have not been forgotten; women scrounging for food and feeding the hungry from big communal pots in the shantytowns; hiding fugitives from the police; presenting petitions and making statements to the United Nations; relentlessly documenting the shame of the dictatorship day after day. They say: "Through joint action we are overcoming the fear that paralyzed us for so long. We have to fight for this just cause in every barrio, in every shantytown, in every village, city and organization. Our determined voice, our responsible action, will attract many more voices and strengthen our decision to put an end to the black night of dictatorship. If we are few on the street today, tomorrow there should be millions here with us."[12]

In my experience this message exemplifies the feelings of the majority of women in Chile today. Their lives have been turned upside down by the dictatorship. The nightmarish litany is now familiar: arrest, torture, disappearance, death, exile, hunger, constant terror. The scenes that come to life on the arpilleras are so terrifying because they are real, they are not imagined, they are made of flesh and blood.

Anita, whose son was arrested and disappeared in 1974, is one of the original members of the group and one of the most active and dedicated. She says: "I started to make arpilleras based on my grief and my anguish. It was a way we found of alleviating our pain because we could tell our story and at the same time denounce what happened to us."[13]

As I leave Chile, I leave behind the volatile images, fragile as the women's white hankerchiefs waving near prisons and torture centres, hiding tears during uncertain farewells. I see the phantasmal and lucid figures of these women on their constant pilgrimages, women I have come to know during the hours we spent together, hours so intensely emotional that ordinary time becomes an inadequate measure. Something of them has penetrated my skin, my eyes, changed my vision of the world. At night I think of them, I remember them, I feel them nearby and I hear their determined steps on their trek through the morgues and the prisons of the imprisoned country. At times in my dreams I see them laying flowers on imaginary graves; other times I see them knitting socks to be ready for the return, cleaning the uninhabited room to keep it ready for the return, working in the garden because he loved to sit there to watch butterflies and days flutter by. I am now linked to them by some process of which I am uncertain, perhaps by sharing their pain, or because of my desire to know the truth of their lives, or perhaps because we are all women, because we all belong to a group that history has generally consigned to silence. But now our own history obliges us to speak, to loose words of fire. Thus we come out of the silence and darkness to show ourselves as we are: free women, fighting women. We are washers of clothes, teachers, lawyers, journalists, poets. We are mothers, sisters, wives, daughters. We throw ourselves into the abyss of uncertainties with new-found strength; we are not afraid to dive into the hell of lies, into the visible and invisible machinations of the dictatorship. We wage our war every day in the country called Chile or Guatemala or the United States. We are new women with new stories to tell.

Back at my home in the United States, I open the secret present given to me by my friends at the airport just before I left. It is an arpillera with a blue sky and the open pages of a letter flying through the air, pages carrying the story that I now pass on to you.

FOOTNOTES

1　The curfew was imposed from 1973 through 1975 and again afterwards during periods when it was considered necessary "for the security of the country." In 1984 it was reimposed and remains in effect today.

2　Almost all the information in this article comes from my personal experiences with the Association of Families of the Detained-Disappeared and from previous information supplied by the Vicarate of Solidarity in 1975 and 1976, entitled *Informes (Report)*. Also see the book by Hernán Vidal, *Dar la Vida por la Vida (Give Life for Life)*, Institute for the Study of Ideologies and Literature, Minneapolis, Minnesota, 1982, a very complete book concerning the various activities of the Association, particularly the public protests.

3　*Desapareciones (Disappearance*　Editorial Fundamentos Amnestía Internacional, Madrid, Spain, 1984, p.9.

3a *Nunca Más (Never Again)*, I port of the Sábato Commission, Barcelona, Seix Barral, 1983.

4　Hernán Vidal, p.59.

5　For more information on the disappearances exclusively in Chile, see ¿ Dónde están? (Where are They?), Vicaria de la Solidaridad, Santiago de Chile, and *The Pinochet Decade*, Latin American Bureau, London, England, 1983.

6　Information supplied by Irma, member of the Association.

7　Vidal, p.114. For a detailed analysis of the incident of Lonquén, see Máximo Pacheco, *Lonquén*. Santiago: Editorial Aconcagua, 1980.

8　Vidal, p.96.

9　Vidal, p.167.

10 For a detailed article on the arpilleras, see Marjorie Agosin, "Needles That Talk: The Chilean Arpilleras." In: *International Journal of Women's Studies*, Vol. 7, no. 2. Montreal: Eden Press, March/April, 1984, pp. 173-178.

11 For information on the behaviour of women in Latin American prisons in countries living under dictatorships, see Chapter III of Luis Vitale in *Historia y Sociología de la mujer latinoamericana* (History and Sociology of the Latin American Woman). Madrid: Editorial Fundamentos and Barcelona: Fontamara, 1981.

12 Fragments of the article of Ximena Bunster, "Women's Resistance to Pinochet and Their Struggle for a Return to Democracy." In: *Cultural Survival Quarterly*, Vol. 8, no. 2, Summer 1984, p.64.

13 Most of the information in this article comes from my own personal experiences and from interviews with women of the Association of Families of the Detained-Disappeared during 1984.

CHAPTER 2

CHILEAN WOMEN, POLITICS AND SOCIETY: 1971-1984

As part of my preparation for this book, I made an intensive search for specific materials dealing with the participation of Chilean women in the political development of the country. The information I was able to find was so scanty, so poorly documented, that I realized my first task would be to try to reconstruct a history already almost lost, particularly since women's role under the dictatorship becomes more and more secondary and hidden.[1]

In this chapter I will attempt to describe the main elements of the feminist movement in Chile, its principal successes, such as gaining the right of women to vote (in 1949), the role of Chilean women during the Socialist government of Salvador Allende (1971-1973), and finally I will show how women were cleverly manipulated by the right wing opposition into playing a major role in the overthrow of Allende, making way for the military Junta that still rules Chile today.

The countries of Latin America spent many years fighting wars of independence from Spain, searching for their own freedom and autonomy, but the women of the continent seem to have been absent from that long struggle. If they did take part, their participation has not been recorded. We are left to conclude that each woman was restricted to her own household, to the care of her own family.

The feminist movement arose very late in Chile in comparison to countries of the west, and only began to attract popular support in the 1920s and 1930s. At that time groups of women, mostly from the upper class, began meeting together in each other's homes in so-called *Círculos de Señoras* (Women's Circles), modelled on the women's Reading Clubs then widespread in the United States, to discuss how they could participate more fully in the civic and cultural life of the country. It is a curious paradox that women in Chile were allowed to attend universities very early. The University of Chile accepted women as early as 1800. The first woman doctor graduated in 1886 and the first lawyer in 1892.[2] (For more information see Klimpel and Kirkwood, p.168). The Women's Circles began to try to win entry into political life as one of their first efforts. In 1917 they petitioned the parliament for the right to vote. In 1919 they organized the Women's Civic Party. This was not a true political party, in that women did not yet have the right to vote, but it was a way of focussing attention on political events from women's point of view. Women first gained the right to vote in municipal elections in 1931.[3] The period of greatest political fervour occurred between 1920-1940, but the women's movement was still very much a movement of the upper class.

As late as the 1940s women in Chile, from a legal point of view, amounted to very little more than another possession for a man's house. This situation is best illustrated by quoting from legislation of the 19th century that makes it very clear that married women were considered the property of the husband. "The husband has the right to oblige his wife to live with him and to follow him wherever he may wish to reside....In addition the act of marriage merges the properties of both parties and the administration of the common property becomes the right of the husband." The same law goes on to say: "Without written authorization by the husband the married woman cannot make decisions on her own, not even through a lawyer, nor is she allowed to sign any sort of contract or withdraw from a contract signed at an earlier date." (Klimpel). Women were not allowed to make any decision regarding the property of their children, and had no say in the education of their children. According to Serrano laws governing the rights of women have not changed very much. The major changes are as follows: adoption of the concept of equal pay for equal work, provision of public day care facilities, the right to maternity leave (six weeks before birth and three months afterwards). Before these reforms were passed in 1925, a woman could not work without authorization of her husband; that provision no longer exists. We should point out that many of these rights have been lost under the dictatorship. Now pregnant women may be fired with impunity because of their condition, although there is still no legal abortion in Chile (never has been) and abortion remains the number one cause of maternal death according to Weisner.[4]

A problem still crucial in Chile now approaching the end of the 20th century concerns the very different education offered to women and men. For the most part boys and girls are educated separately, and in the girls' schools, academic subjects give way to "feminine" subjects: lady-like skills such as needlework, a little music, a little art, practical instruction in how to run a household, essentially how to be a good wife with a little extra polish. But as it turned out the traditional skills of sewing and embroidering are the ones the Chilean arpilleristas adopted for their ongoing fight against the military dictatorship.

The first stirrings of the feminist movement coincided with the beginning of the industrial revolution in Chile, about 1915, when women were required as part of the labour force in the new industrial mills and plants. Leaving the home and working alongside men began a new epoch for Chilean women. They were naturally caught up in the nationwide changes that occurred as the society started to shift from primarily agrarian to an urban, industrialized society. By 1915 almost 40 percent of the population was already living in cities where the factories and mills were located. Most of the women workers of the time were employed in sewing plants attached to textile mills.

As for the feminist movement itself, it was marked by three distinct phases: the period of formation, the period of isolated struggles, and the period of coordinated action followed by disintegration.[5] The drive for equal opportunity for women came, as said earlier, from the upper class and was at the express initiative of the great educator, Amanda Labarca. It was Labarca who adopted the idea of Reading Clubs from the United States and formed similar clubs in Chile. Many important and well-known women attended meetings of these clubs, including Gabriela Mistral, the poet who was awarded the Nobel Prize for Literature in 1945. Newspapers and magazines began to publish writings of some of the talented and outstanding women of those years. Coming together in the clubs allowed a certain solidarity and sense of common purpose to develop among the women.[6]

The Women's Circles and Reading Clubs were attacked by reactionaries who did not wish women to step out of their traditional roles, and it goes without saying that many husbands opposed their wives' wishes for more independence.

In 1917 the Reading Clubs were supplanted by the newly-formed Consejo Nacional de Mujeres (The National Council of Women). It was then they presented their first petition asking for the right to vote. The language of the petition was humble and not at all aggressive. From this modest opening, the campaign for women's suffrage began growing in strength and importance. A number of congresses in different parts of the country were organized to push for women's suffrage legislation. More than two decades later, in 1949, by official decree, Chilean women finally won the right to vote. Although this was only the first step in satisfying the desires of women for affirmation of their rights as individuals in many other areas of life, the momentum of the movement stopped with the obtaining of suffrage. A Feminist Party was formed in 1948,[7] led by María de la Cruz, and its platform was unique for its progressive ideas, but unfortunately it was unable to keep women united and was dissolved in 1951 because of internal tensions that have never been completely revealed to this day.

In general, social movements arise when demands are not met through regular legal or constitutional channels. That is certainly the case of the members of the Association of the Families of the Detained-Disappeared in Chile today. So it was that after women received the right to vote, their movement withered away. Many members of the various feminist groups involved in the suffrage fight were incorporated into the traditional political parties, naturally dominated by men and reflecting men's interests. Women thus returned to their position in the background of history, to their second class role. The movement of the arpilleristas offers interesting contrasts to the old feminist movement, in that the arpilleristas have not joined any political parties as a way of furthering their aims. They are working outside the traditional political system to effect political change. And of course a fundamental difference is that the arpillerista movement is completely a women's movement; there are no men involved. It is run entirely by women.

Another aspect that might explain the disintegration of the feminist movement in Chile lies in its political make-up, the pluralism of its membership and the integration within the membership of women of all different social classes. This means that after winning suffrage, women of different social and economic strata had different needs and desires, totally different sets of problems. Another factor to consider is that women activists wished to participate in national life not to obtain power and prestige for themselves, but to benefit their children and larger segments of the population in need of help. They were not working for drastic change but for modification of the existing system. This altruistic thrust of the feminist movement in Chile makes it very different from the feminist movements in western countries. In Chile women have been more concerned with the problems of class than those of sexual identity. Since Chile is essentially an oligarchy the separation of classes is a fundamental part of the system.

According to what I have been able to ascertain from the few records available to me, covering the years since 1949, we have to conclude that during those years women have essentially been excluded from the official levels of government. There is now a tenuous resurgence of the type of feminist movement that won suffrage for women. Various groups of women throughout the country have come together under the umbrella organization known as MEMCH, Movimiento de Emancipación de la Mujer Chilena (Movement for the Liberation of Chilean Women). MEMCH was formed in 1936, and as part of its program advocated legal divorce, lobbied for standardized pay for female domestic servants (their pay to be equal to the pay for men servants), and asserted women's need to organize in autonomous women's organizations. This emphasis on autonomy from traditional political parties has been a very important part of the MEMCH ideology. According to Covarrubias, Chilean feminism disappeared after 1940, and MEMCH as well, because most women had gravitated to the regular political parties by then, (p.162). Now MEMCH is enjoying a revival. It was reconstituted in 1983 and called a public forum to organize women to fight against the pervasive male domination of Chilean society.

When we think of women and the Socialist movement, we might assume that there was a natural inclination in favour of women's equality. However, we find this was not the case in Chile. Again the task of investigating the role of women in the Chilean Socialist movement is very difficult. I have found very little literature on the subject.

Elsa Chaney, in her book *Supermadre* (Supermother)[8], says that her research concerning the participation of women in politics in Chile shows that women tend to take on the role of Supermother; that is, their participation in public life has consisted of a re-emphasis of feminine concerns, such as better schools for the children, day care centres and so forth. Chaney says: "In spite of abundant socialist rhetoric on the necessity for complete equality of men and women in building a socialist society, the Latin American male is macho first and político second. Hence he expects very little shoulder-to-shoulder comradeship from the women of his party. There are outstanding exceptions, but on the whole, the few Communist and Socialist women in public office, define their political role in terms of 'support' of the male and concentrate on typical feminine activities within their parties. This is true even though leftist parties in Latin America do not generally segregate women into separate feminine sections. But home and family responsibilities typically are put first even by the women of the left in Chile and Peru."[9]

Chaney's statistics indeed support the theory that women's participation in politics is behind the scenes and therefore invisible. Again we see the arpilleristas overturning all the traditional stereotypes. Women in Chile, most especially the arpilleristas who belong to the Association of the Families of the Detained-Disappeared, represent the only part of the population that has been able to organize and make *public* protests against the dictatorship. Their unity is holding in spite of the fact that they include women of varying political views. I have attended meetings and heard discussions between women who regard themselves as Communist, Socialist, or Christian Democrat, but above all as a member of the Association and as an arpillerista. Now there are more open protests by students, young people, labour union members, and others, but the police deal with them much more harshly than they do with women-mothers. During the work stoppages and demonstrations of early July, 1986, police with painted faces (so they could not be recognized) actually doused two teenagers with gasoline and set them afire. One died a few days later; a month later the other is still hospitalized.

This difference in treatment of women is a common phenomenon throughout Latin America, and taking advantage of it, women have moved into public spaces formerly closed to them, such as streets and plazas, although they have no legal voice within the Chilean opposition. The male population in Chile has been decimated as in a war, by prison, exile and disappearances, leaving an empty terrain for women to take over as their own. The men who are free are kept under such tight control by the Junta that their opportunities for action have been drastically reduced. So the arpilleristas have proven that women can take advantage of their assigned role and use it to fight for justice for their children first of all, but also for wider social reforms. It is indeed a paradox that the machista view of women has allowed them to enter the political sphere, and at a time when practically all channels for political action have been effectively closed for men.

Perhaps the scant participation granted to women by Allende's Socialist government, his treatment of women in general, the fact that their voices were not heard in Party or Government affairs, that he did not publicly espouse a more egalitarian conception of the world, cost him the support of many women. There is no doubt that

25

many fought actively against him, joined the right-wing conspiracy that brought about his overthrow. It is quite easy to distinguish the political complexion of Chilean women, because votes by men and women are counted separately.[10] I have been unable to find any document that would provide a rationale for the extraordinary fact that even polling places for men and women are separate. To quote Kyle and Francis: "Men and women vote in different polling places and their respective totals are recorded separately. This, coupled with Chile's reliable census data, frequent elections, and wide spectrum of political choices, provides a rare opportunity to isolate and discuss the voting patterns of women."

In any case this circumstance makes it possible to speculate about what role women played in the 1970 election (Allende, United Popular Front against Frei, Christian Democrats). Although women cast 50 percent of the vote, this high count does not translate into real political participation. According to some published polls, the act of voting is not viewed by women as a method of political power, but rather as a civic duty, to set a good example by taking an interest in national life, particularly as it affects the welfare of their children and households. (See Chaney, *The Mobilization of Women in Allende's Chile*). For whatever reason, Allende's administration never seemed to take the support of women seriously. No coherent effort was ever made to use feminine supporters in a dynamic, constructive way. As Chaney points out: "Nowhere else in the world have events conspired to make women's political participation so vital an issue as in Chile."[11] We know for certain that women's vote on the whole was strongly inclined toward support of the political right.

Chaney quotes Allende as saying: "All the elections we lost because of the women's vote. It is our fault because we haven't found out how to reach the consciousness and hearts of women. There is still prejudice among the men of the United Popular Front." In that statement Allende was referring in particular to the elections of 1958 when he lost to Jorge Alesandri, who won by a margin of 33,000 votes. Twelve years later women again failed to vote for Allende in sufficient numbers in the elections of 1970. Even women of the poor, marginal neighbourhoods in Santiago, in general, have held a conservative political point of view. I believe this is not due to a thought-out political philosophy, but is rather a fear of any change that might threaten their traditional way of life, the world they are used to. It is curious, though, that in periods of real political upheaval, women, particularly poor and working-class women, have shown they are capable of creative political action, and not just in the usual areas of home and children. At times they have assumed true leadership positions in organizations in their own neighbourhoods, proving they are capable of exercising leadership. It is a fact of history that they have been excluded from government and party positions in Chile, and not from some defect in their make-up.

In his speeches Allende always referred to the importance of women and to how much they were helping to bring about social and cultural change within the country. However, his brief term in office was notable for the absence of women in high positions. Only after he had been in office for two years did he appoint a woman, only one, to a Cabinet position, a typical "woman's" post, as head of the Social Development Agency. Not even the women who had fought so militantly for him within the Socialist Party and the MAPU (Movimiento de Acción Popular/Movement of Popular Action) were included in leadership positions in any of the different agencies set up by Allende.[12]

So Allende's greatest mistake may have been that of underestimating the potential of Chilean women. Sounding exactly like any traditional bourgeois male, he said he valued the Chilean woman as mother above anything else. To quote Chaney again, Allende said: "When I say woman I always think of the woman-mother. When I talk of woman, I refer to her function in the nuclear family.... The child is the prolongation of the woman who in essence is born to be a mother." It is not surprising that the projects proposed by the Allende government having to do with women remained within the typically feminine perimeters. To be fair, other liberal projects were proposed but could never be financed, because of economic problems.

Allende's efforts to do something for women were like his

speeches: intended to keep her in the domestic work force but to ease her lot a little and in addition to make provisions for her old age when she could no longer work. But for all his own failings toward women, he did not hesitate to lecture the men in his audiences on the subject. In one speech he chided them saying: "Men have the obligation of understanding women and of making themselves understood....You all go to the demonstrations alone; you don't ever bring your wives along. You go home and don't talk to them. You never say, look here, and you should dialogue with the women." (Quotation taken from Chaney).

There seems no doubt that Salvador Allende himself sincerely intended to incorporate women into his government, but he was never able to go beyond the prevailing traditional, clearly male ideology of the society. He was prevented from launching several progressive projects because of severe economic problems. The only programs that took on a certain momentum were the domestic ones developed in the Centros de Madres (Mothers' Centres) where sewing, knitting and other home crafts were taught. It was these same programs that later spawned the idea for the Chilean arpillera workshops. It is sad to think that it was the men of the United Popular Front who more than anyone else brought about their own downfall, by being unable to rid themselves or their political movement of the pervasive machismo of the society. This attitude is clearly illustrated by the leftist press, which continued to reinforce the idea of woman-as-sexual-object-only. Mira Bambirra points out that many leftist publications supporting Allende constantly printed cartoons showing politically activist women with bared legs and breasts.[13]

We may conclude that the Chilean Socialist Party failed by ignoring half of the electorate. Even militant political parties were not any more enlightened; women were (and still are) included only as adjuncts to the dominant males. We believe the experience of the Chilean Socialists clearly demonstrates that there can be no meaningful social reforms for women if the changes proposed are to be implemented by the same age-old system from which women are excluded as equal partners.

Orchestrating Allende's Downfall

It has been well documented that the severe shortages of foodstuffs and other household necessities that occurred during Allende's government were due to two main causes: hoarding by the affluent (and prudent) upper class and the strikes of transport workers. To add to the economic crisis, there was a fall in the price of copper, strikes by miners, and behind and beneath all this, the constant and determined machinations of the United States to destablize the government. It is clear that Allende's government was not to be given the chance to survive.

We have to wonder what might have happened if Allende had known how to rally large numbers of women in the political process. The result of all this was that the only women who were free and had the time to become politically involved, the only ones *asked* to become politically invoved, were the women of the middle and upper class. Some of them made contacts with poor women, wives of strikers in particular, and they all worked for the opposition, against Allende. Early in 1971 the women of the upper classes began an effective concerted action: they began the famous marches banging empty pots. Naturally the women chose for their symbol a strictly feminine household object. Nevertheless, they did abandon their passive role to embark on a more active phase of their lives by going out into the streets to march and demand change. So began a new chapter in the history of Chilean politics: the manipulation of women for political purposes by right-wing groups.

Michelle Mattelart in a brilliant article, "Cuando las mujeres salen a la calle" (When the Women Go Out into the Street) [14] analyzes with consumate skill the problems faced by women of the bourgeoisie in Chile, and we will use her analysis as background for this discussion. Any political history of Latin American women will have to take into account their conservatism, which we mentioned earlier, an attitude that cuts across all class lines. It is a fact that throughout history Latin American women have resisted rather than welcomed change. When we consider the organized demands of housewives in Brazil and Guatemala for equal treatment and freedom, we note that the participants do not include working women or women from the country. The movements come from intellectuals and educated women. Only in Nicaragua do we hear of working and farm women participating in various movements, but we have too little information to know how the movements arose and how they are structured. However, the arpilleristas movement is made up of women from the lower and middle class, and is therefore more eclectic in its membership than other groups we have been able to examine.

The true agents of change in Chile in the early 1970s were women, mostly from the middle class, who were caught up in a political tide controlled by right-wing political groups. The so-called movement of the marches of the empty pots, so visible and effective, was carried out by women who were really apolitical, many of whom actually disapproved of political activism for women. These are the same women who took along their maids to protest with them in the first famous march. Now the women who bang the pots do so to demonstrate true need, the grinding hunger and poverty that haunts the streets and alleyways of the shantytowns.

To quote Mallelart once again: "Once we saw the Chilean women marching, we knew Allende's days were numbered." A similiar statement was made by a member of the Brazilian military, an engineer, who said: "We taught the Chileans to use their women against the Marxists....Women constitute the most efficient political weapon; they have time, they are capable of great emotion and they can mobilize quickly. For instance if you want to start a rumour that the President drinks too much, or that he has serious health problems, use women.... By the next day the rumour will be all over the country."[15]

This type of cynical manipulation of women did in fact happen in Chile and helped to bring Pinochet to power. The day after the coup Pinochet publicly and pointedly thanked women for their help in the "battle for democracy." The same rhetoric is still being used: women are the "pillars" that support the "reconstruction" of the country. (As long as they are not perceived as opposing the Junta of course; in that case, women are arrested, raped, tortured and disappeared — not treated like men prisoners but worse). However, Pinochet's fullsome praise of women for their help in "reconstructing the country" (the Junta's expression) has caused many women to feel a real devotion to him, such as a loyal subject might feel toward a benevolent monarch.

In her chilling book, *Miedo en Chile* (Fear in Chile) Patricia Politzer includes an interview with a woman named Raquel, a Pinochet supporter all the way, according to what she herself says. She describes her feelings this way: "He (Pinochet) and Señora Lucía are very nice people, the most unassuming people in the world. The first time I saw him was when he visited the población of Zajón de la Aguada. The women adored him, they kissed his hands, they were so happy and appreciative. I have never had one moment's doubt about him."[16] (Zajón de la Aguada is a marginal satellite township north of Santiago that might be characterized as a very modest working-class quarter. The city has built some public housing; there is running water and electricity. It is by no means one of the poorest of the marginal towns, and there was little opposition to Pinochet here).

It is revealing to compare this statement of Raquel's with one made by Moy de Tohá, wife of José Tohá, minister of defense in Allende's administration who died in exile on Dawson Island. (Dawson Island, located near the 53rd parallel south, just east of the main island of Tierra del Fuego, is one of the remote locations used by the Junta as a place of internal exile, where concentration camps have been built for political prisoners). Just after the coup Moy Tohá was on very friendly terms with Pinochet, but after her husband was arrested and sent into exile, and she was allowed to go visit him, her attitude changed. She described what it was like to live among the military: "I began to feel that we were in the hands of irrational butchers whose behaviour could not be foreseen, calculated or controlled.... For them (the military) women are second-class beings, delicate and fragile, that must always be treated like ladies. That's how it was every time we had to talk to them, obviously I mean women who were not prisoners, because they had no problem leaving us for twenty days or more under house arrest so we couldn't go anywhere."[17]

These two statements show two extreme opposite attitudes of women toward Pinochet and the military, which brings us to the complex nature of the relationship of women to politics in Chile. The reader may have received the impression from what has been said before in this chapter that only members of the less privileged classes of society supported Allende, but this is not the case. There are many factors that influence women's political choices. To quote Julieta Kirkwood, "The social and political condition of women is due fundamentally to the social insertion of the individual woman, the form in which she is involved or not in the culture of her time, to her marginal position or not, to her civilization and her surroundings, to her comprehension of the general interests of the society...."[18] Many women of the upper class supported the Socialist government and many poor women from shantytowns and marginal neighbourhoods supported the traditional, patriarchal society represented by Pinochet. However, we should keep in mind that in Chile, in general, the woman is regarded as the mainstay, the major social force governing the home, the major socializing force, and most men respect her power in that area but are unwilling to allow her to move out of her traditional territory to a wider sphere. As we have seen, the government of Allende made no attempt to change matters as far as women's role went. She was confined to areas considered proper for her, was not encouraged to participate in political activities, or in any other activities outside the home. This attitude is not limited to one party or one country, as Mattelart points out, but is the usual one throughout Latin America. The arpilleristas, at least, seem to have found a way not around the attitude but to use the attitude. They perceived that since they are mothers in a system that only allows them to be mothers, they would use their very conditions as mothers as their prime political weapon. The ultra machista regime of the Junta finds itself in a real bind as to how to deal with them.

But to go back a bit, the first dramatic political action taken by women occurred immediately after Allende's election. On the night of December 1, 1971, the first march with the empty pots occurred.

Women, mostly of the affluent upper class, came into the streets banging pots and proclaiming their disapproval of the election results. As we said earlier many women marched accompanied by their maids. We know now that the women were organized and directed by a group of the extreme right called Patria y Libertad (Country and Freedom). Later this same organization took control of the movement called Poder Femenino (Feminine Power). Women were recruited by the right wing for other demonstrations as well, such as to go in groups to Allende's office to ask him to resign.

As we indicated above, most of the women in these early anti-Allende demonstrations were affluent and well-to-do. There were very few women of the working class to be found among them. Their participation came later as a result of the strikes. When the strikes of miners and truck drivers began — strikes that were fomented by the oligarchy and the CIA — wives of striking workers were aided by women of the right wing to organize and provision community soup kitchens. The sight of the open air soup pots and lines of hungry men and children was designed to arouse sympathy and feelings of solidarity for the workers, all emotions directed against Allende, of course. This part of the Allende story has been well documented in several excellent studies. [19]

The combination of the suffering of the working people and their families, the supposedly empty pots of the bourgeoisie, all the shortages, produced a chaotic, out-of-control atmosphere in Chile, as was intended. As time went on women in the poor neighbourhoods, who had no food hoarded to fall back on, were reduced to pooling their scant food supply in order to have a little for everybody, and they were aided by women of Feminine Power, a ploy intended to draw the strikers' wives into the active anti-Allende campaign.

The old equations — woman-housewife, woman-mother, mother-country — remained the same as women were manipulated into helping bring about the overthrow of Allende and his United Popular Front Government. Women remained in their secondary, background role, thus bringing to an end a progressive movement begun by the Christian Democratic Government of Eduardo Frei which had begun to draw women into public life in a wider and more meaningful way. After the coup there were to be no more women in power. The women of the bourgeoisie were buried under a barrage of propaganda. The real problems of the country were forgotten, and the discourse concerning women turned completely traditional and apolitical: home, family, country, and the need of the country for a responsible "father": Pinochet, of course. The Reading Circles started years ago by Amanda Labarca went back to discussing the same things they had discussed in their beginning. What might have been an effective movement for women's liberation, begun in 1964 under the Christian Democrats and which might have been expected to be broadened and invigorated under the United Popular Front, came to nothing. The Mothers' Centres, begun under Frei, were taken over by the Junta for their own uses as we shall discuss in more detail in the next chapter. It suffices to say here that the Junta's approach to the Mothers' Centres was to institute a system that combined indoctrination, work and benefits coupled with the threat of withdrawing work and benefits and perhaps imposing reprisals as well at the sign of any restiveness or independent action on the part of any woman. Thus the militarization of the entire country was completed, from the highest levels down to the lowliest household. The takeover was so complete that it led Pinochet to boast later, "Not a leaf falls in this country that I don't know about."[20]

There are only a few essays that treat the subject of the manipulation of women by the political right wing in any kind of serious way. However, there are a number of accounts about the period written by women who were involved in the right wing movement.[21] It would be interesting to see a comparison made of the language of the slogans used by right-wing women in their campaigns and that of the slogans of the arpilleristas that appeared later. To give one example, in 1971 and 1972, the women of the right were carrying signs that said, "WHAT HAVE THEY DONE WITH OUR CARS?" After 1973 the posters of the arpilleristas read: "BREAD FOOD WORK FREEDOM" or the starkest of all: "WHERE ARE THEY?" referring to the *disappeared*.

There is one book of the political right called *La guerra de las mujeres* (The War of the Woman) (cited in Footnote 21), published (ironically enough) by the press of the National Technical University, one of the universities of the country that tried to incorporate workers into their classes during the Allende years. The book describes the struggle of women against the elected government of Allende, with special attention being paid to the women who operated under the protection of the paramilitary organization, Patria y Libertad (Country and Freedom) mentioned earlier. The style of the book is not easy to describe. The language is superficial, chatty, and appears to try to reproduce what the author thought was typical housewife chitchat, but the quotes are obviously from privileged upper-class women, exalted by the fact that they were involved in a titanic revolutionary struggle against the dark forces of Marxism. Here are a few quotes from the book: "The rebellion was of such a great magnitude that the Government (of Allende) tried to stop it. The entire citizenry participated in this fight to defend the youth and the rights of parents to educate their children...." And note the following statement about education under Allende: "The public and private schools were forced to impress young minds with violent films that showed the most awful misery, specifically intended to disturb impressionable young minds with dangerous distortions of cause and effect. At that time (during Allende's time in office) history itself has been changed, even some phrases of the national anthem that speak of liberty for the country."[23]

We indicated earlier in this chapter how women of the bourgeoisie gained support of women of the working class. Morandé says, "From the beginning the members of Feminine Power approached wives of striking miners, offering them food and moral support. On many occasions the long battle weighed heavy on the spirits of the rough mountain men. Then their wives took up the banner. They always came up with some idea, some action, that encouraged the men. The women's voices gave strength and courage to the men, fostering a climate of sharp resistance....Feminine Power was on constant call to help women all over the country. From many different places they were always calling asking to speak to the women in the headquarters."[24]

Notice that this Feminine Power, part of a concrete system, with a complex and widespread organization was totally under the direction of another power, that of the masculine right, Country and Freedom. *The War of the Women* deals with different aspects of the mobilization of large segments of the country by the right to bring about the overthrow of Allende. The language in the sections regarding poor women and wives of striking workers who were involved in the effort is somewhat vulgar and patronizing, in spite of the fact that these women played an important role for the right.

As a counterbalance to this sort of propaganda and the image of women clung to in a neurotic way by the present Junta, we have the vigorous response of the arpilleristas. Their response is in their work, a unique expression born entirely of their own consciences and sensibilities — their stories presented as graphically as banner headlines in a newspaper. The history they are compiling is not a history of isolated events and dates of a dark period of Chilean history, but is a true and courageous confrontation with concerns of a much deeper level, those of the heart and soul, life and death, evil, grief, sorrow, friendship, work, hope. Now in Chile, women intellectuals and artists are beginning to join with the arpilleristas and other working-class women to search together for a common response to a common dilemma. It is now perceived by a sizeable group of Chilean women that they are all enslaved, sometimes by one another, but all ultimately by a system that is endemically repressive to women.

There are some encouraging first signs of a breaking down of class barriers separating women from one another: the recognition that the traditional view of women fostered by the Junta and those in power is a false one whose purpose is to keep women subjugated, and the recognition that the past, when the image may have had some meaning, is dead and gone. It is to be hoped that a new collective conscience will grow from such insights.

One of the biggest questions facing women is whether to seek liberation by themselves and for themselves, starting on a grass-roots level in order to dissipate the old myths that woman is a passive creature, especially now that one out of every three households in Chile is headed by a woman. In this case the movement for women's liberation would not have to search for highly visible leaders but would begin slowly with small groups that would allow leadership to appear naturally from the now hidden and faceless women. Our history as women is and must be a search to bring to light our history not yet written, still waiting to be told.

Conclusion

We have attempted to show some of the abortive, frustrating, sometimes misguided efforts of women to participate more fully in the national life of Chile, to establish themselves as independent persons, to step out of their roles as shadowy appendages, mothers and wives, domestic labourers. This brief history alone would make the emergence of the arpilleristas in Chile an unusual phenomenon: a group of women working independently and autonomously, even though using such a traditional feminine tool as sewing. The arpilleristas had no long-term plan or strategy in mind when they began. They came together out of drastic need and to seek solace from one another. They were in a precarious economic situation; they were psychologically deeply wounded. They started to make the arpilleras first as a means to earn a little money, but very quickly discovered that the therapeutic value of working together with other women and the resulting community feeling was as valuable as their earnings, perhaps more so. As their psychic wounds began to heal, they began to gain self-confidence, to lose the fear that had paralyzed them, and they started to fight back. They wanted first of all to tell their stories, to let the world know what had happened to them. Their way of fighting back and telling their stories was through their arpilleras. By speaking out in their own way, on their own terms, they stopped being "just" housewives, "just" mothers, and became citizens, members of a wider community, demanding rights and justice for all. It is too early to be able to measure the importance of this movement. So far very little has been written about the arpilleras as a means of political expression, though they have been described as crafts. but no one can fail to see that the arpilleristas are a trail-bl. ing group, an organic entity that grew as naturally as a plant grows and as time went on invented or discovered ways to oppose and elude a system that puts them in second place, leaves them in the shadows. By using the most modest tools imaginable, scraps of left-over cloth, they tell the true stories of their lives, their losses and deaths, their hopes, their agony and that of their country, and they condemn those who have brought about so much misery. Irony of ironies, they have managed to remain a constant irritant to the vaunted, impeturbable Junta. In the next chapter we will describe the various methods the Junta has used to try to silence them, all ineffective so far.

Aside from the arpilleras the history of Chilean women since 1970 to the present has not been told by them. The movement of the arpilleristas, still in its infancy and still to be fully realized, even though it has been in existence for 14 years, is, nevertheless, the first autonomous movement in Chile organized by working-class women. The group includes some women of the middle and upper classes, but it is primarily a movement of women from the marginal areas, women with a long history of being exploited, victimized and oppressed. The arpilleras reveal the oppression they suffer, but the work itself, done individually and in a cooperative spirit with a group, makes a collective response to their imperious problems. By means of their work, the arpilleristas affirm their identity as women, but also as individuals committed to political and social change through cooperative effort.

With all channels of free expression now closed in Chile, the arpilleras take on special significance. They are more than personal statements. They provide a way for their makers to organize and participate in public life at a time when organizing and political action is forbidden; a way to document and denounce oppression when all other forms of documentation and denunciation are censored and banned. The women slip all their bonds when their arpilleras escape across the borders and go winging around the world with their vivid tales, and when the arpilleristas go out unafraid into the street to protest, to demand their rights and to ask for justice for family members wrested from them, justice for anyone who is suffering.

The arpilleras have become explicit, conscious expressions of facts, opinions and feelings. They are the revolutionary banners of present-day Chile. The revolution they proclaim is not based on abstract theory or books but comes out of everyday lives, from a time and space real and precise. Begun as a way to earn money, they have turned into much more, so much more it is difficult to comprehend all the ramifications. For the women who make them, they have opened up a new life — one of self-confident, independent, fearless action. Indeed, what a small group of women in Santiago has accomplished, working so modestly in church basements with scraps of left-over cloth, is a cause for wonder. In the following chapters we will get to know them better. Finally they will tell us their stories in their own words. Perhaps then we can begin to appreciate the true dimensions of their efforts.

FOOTNOTES

1 Books and studies dealing with Chilean women are listed in the bibliography of this book. The most helpful books and studies for this chapter are the following:
, Covarrubias Paz, "El movimiento femenista chileno" (The Chilean Feminist Movement). In: Covarrubias and Franco, eds., *Chile: Mujer y sociedad* (Chile: Woman and Society). Santiago: UNICEF, 1978, pp. 168-648; and the internal documents of the Círculo de Estudios de la mujer for the years 1979-1982. These may be obtained by writing to the headquarters of the Círculo, Purisima 533, Santiago, Chile.

2 For a discussion of women's legal rights see: Felicitas Klimpel, *La mujer chilena: El aporte femenino al progreso de Chile 1910-1960* (The Chilean Woman: Her Contributions to the Progress of Chile 1910-1960). Santiago: Andrés Bello, 1962, p. 63. Also for a new update in changing laws, see Elena Serrano, "La mujer en la legislación chilena" (Woman in Chilean Law), internal report, 1983, published by the Círculo de Estudios de la Mujer. Also see Larraín Rios, "Situación legal de la mujer frente al marido y los hijos" (Legal Situation of the Woman in Relation to Husband and Children). In: Covarrubias and Franco (cited above in Footnote 1), pp. 649-656. See also Zegers and Haino, "La mujer chilean en el siglo XX" (The Chilean Woman in the 20th Century). In: *Tres ensayos sobre la mujer chilena* (Three Essays about the Chilean Woman). Santiago: Editorial Universitaria, 1978, pp. 110-115.

3 Martina Barros, "El voto femenino" (The Feminine Vote). In: *Revista Chilena*, Vol. 1, 19123, p. 39. Also see Covarrubias, cited in Footnote 1 above.

4 Information taken from Ph.D. thesis of Mónica Weisner, Chilean anthropologist, called *Aborto Inducido: Estudio antropológico en mujeres de bajo nivel socioecónomico* (Induced Abortion: Anthropological Study of Women of Low Socioeconomic Level), 1982.

5 Covarrubias, p. 620.

6 For further information on the Reading Circles, see the essay of one of the founders, Amanda Labarca, "Femenismo contemporáneo" (Contemporary Feminism). Santiago: Zig Zag, 1945, and the new book that studies the Chilean feminist movement from its beginning, La mujer nueva (The New Woman), MEMCH Antología, Ediciones Minga, 1985.

7   The few references to the Partido Femenino Chileno can be found in the book by Klimpel (Footnote 2), pp. 25-35, and in *La mujer nueva* (Footnote 5), p. 52.

8   Elsa Chaney, *Supermadre* (Supermother). Austin: University of Texas Press, 1979, p. 34.

9   Ibid. p. 35.

10 For further information on this subject see Patricia Kyle, "Women at the Polls: The Case of Chile.: In: *Comparative Political Studies, 11, No. 3, October, 1978, pp. 291-310, and Elsa Chaney, "The Mobilization of Women in Allende's Chile." In: Jane Jacquette, Women and Politics.* New York: John Wiley and Sons, 1979. Also see B. Vélez, *Women's Political Behaviour in Chile*, M.A. Thesis, University of California, Berkeley, 1975.

11 Information taken from Chaney. Also see Julieta Kirkwood, "La mujer en la formulación política en Chile." In: Santiago: *Flasco publication, 1979. Internal Report.*

12 *Chaney, Mobilization* p. 52.

13 Mira Bambirra, "Women's Liberation and Class Struggle." In: *The Review of Radical Political Economics* Number 4 Volume 3, pp. 75-84.

14 Most of the information for this section was taken from "Cuando las mujeres salen a la calle" (When the Women Go Out into the Streets). In: *La Cultura de la Opresión Femenina.* México: Ediciones Era, 1977. Also see "The Feminine Version of the coup d'etat." In: Nash and Safa, *Sex and Class in Latin America.* Brooklyn: New York Bergin Publishers.

15 "The Brazilian Connection." *Washington Post*, January 6, 1974.

16 Patricia Politzer, *Miedo en Chile* (Fear in Chile). Santiago: Ediciónes Chile y América, 1984 p. 20.

17 Ibid. p. 334.

18 Julieta Kirkwood, "La formación de la consciencia feminista en Chile" (The forming of a Feminist Conscience in Chile). Santiago: *Flasco* publication, No. 7, 1980. Internal report.

19 Essays by Michelle Mattelart as follows: "Femenismo Balaguerists: A Strategy of the Right." NACLA, Latin American Report Vol. VIII, No. 4, April, 1974; "El nivel mítico de la prensa femenina" (The Mythical Level of the Feminist Press). In: *Cuadernos de la Realidad Nacional.* Santiago: Chile, No. 2, March, 1970; "Apuntes sobre lo moderno: Una manera de leer el magazine; (Notes About the Modern: A Way to Read a Magazine). In: *Casa de las Américas*, March-April, 1973.

20 *El Mercurio.* Santiago, Chile, September 23, 1973, p. 17.

21 The best discussions of the media's role in mobilizing the right wing may be found in the following publications: Armand Mattelart, "Medios masivos de comunicación ideológicas y movimientos revolucionarios" (Mass Media of Ideological Communication and Revolutionary Movements). Paris: Anthropos, 1974; speech by the wife of Pinochet, Lucía Pinochet, "The Mothers of Chile." In: *La Tercera de la Hora*, Santiago de Chile, September 23, 1973, p. 31 and the best source of all, María Correa Morandé, *La guerra de las mujeres* (The War of the Women). Editorial Técnica del Estado, Santiago, 1975.

22 Morandé (Footnote 21), p. 35.

23 Personal information. The old line in the anthem said, "O el asilo contra la opresión" (Oh the haven against oppression) and was changed to, "Chile: copia feliz del Edeń" (Chile: Happy copy of Eden).

24 Morandé (Footnote 21), p. 38.

CHAPTER 3

FORMATION AND BIRTH OF THE WORKSHOPS

By now it is a well-known fact that the military coup that occurred in Chile on September 11, 1973 fell heaviest on the poorest of the population, those living in shantytowns surrounding Santiago and other urban centres. As a result the people in most distress streamed to the churches in search of help, most especially for help in finding out what had happened to family members who had been arrested and taken away by the military.[1] On October 6, 1973 various ecumenical groups met together at the instigation of and under the sponsorship of Cardinal Silva Henríquez for the purpose of creating an organization that would have as its primary concern the protection of human rights, that were then — as well as now — so flagrantly violated by the Chilean military Junta.[2]

During the latter half of September and October 1973, some 7000 people were detained by the Junta and it is only at the end of December that same year that a committee was finally formed to look into the fate of those who had been arrested and were still unaccounted for, still missing.[3] During all this time their families had been unable to learn anything about their whereabouts. The practice of arresting people and having them disappear into the prison system or forever, by killing them and disposing of their bodies in some secret way, still persists in Chile today.

The committee to look into the fate of the *disappeared* was set up with the help of the Catholic Church but functioned as an independent agency. It was made up of representatives of the

Catholic Church, the Methodists, Evangelicals, Lutherans, Pentecostal Christians, and the Jewish community.

So the Pro-Paz (For Peace) Committee was born with the immediate objective of lending support to those whose human rights had been violated. The people involved in forming the Committee never thought then that it would turn into one of the most essential pillars of support to protect the integrity and lives of a large segment of Chilean citizens. Thus the Catholic Church in Chile discovered it had embarked on a task unique in its history. The traditional position of the Catholic Church has almost always been on the side of conservative political parties, an attitude that stems from the period of discovery, conquest, and colonization when the Church was an integral part of the Spanish Empire. During the period we are speaking of, various bishops and other members of the Church hierarchy made public statements approving the overthrow of the Allende Government.[4] Many of them, like many people in the population as a whole, regarded the overthrow as necessary to liberate the country from Marxism. But on the other hand there were other religious leaders who did not offer an explicit legitimacy to the Military Junta, opting instead for a position of official cordiality in order to maintain lines open for dialogue until the country could effect an orderly return to a democratic system.

Although criticism of Pinochet personally was, on the whole, distant and cautious on the part of Church leaders, he was able to count on the support of some very important leaders of the Church.[5] As can be imagined the Pro-Paz Committee was subject to many internal tensions that added complications to their already complicated task. But in spite of difficulties on all sides the group did become organized and went valiantly to work. This was entirely new terrain for the ecumenical group. Instead of joint prayers and workshop services, theological and philosophical discussions, they were working in very concrete ways to try to solve basic problems for their parishioners. By putting themselves publicly and whole-heartedly on the side of the people suffering most severely under the Junta, Pro-Paz found its stance amounted to a militant commitment that put the Committee often in direct conflict with the Junta. This happened due to the courageous attitude of Cardinal Raúl Silva Henríquez.

The Pro-Paz Committee was only allowed to remain in operation for two years before it was closed down by order of the Junta. One of the primary concerns of the Committee was for the fate of the detained-disappeared, and to deal with this most urgent problem, they recruited a group of lawyers to conduct legal inquiries and searches. Most of the lawyers worked without fee on behalf of the aggrieved families. In addition, the Committee began to set up soup kitchens in communities especially hard hit by unemployment or arrests and disappearances. In some neighbourhoods the male population was decimated, and those men still living in freedom were more often than not unable to work. The situation was so extreme that sometimes men who had a job were not able to go to work for lack of clothes, shoes, or eyeglasses. Pro-Paz began collections of clothing and other items of basic need that were distributed through various centres. Eyeglasses were of special importance to women, many of whom suddenly found themselves transformed overnight into heads of households, and they turned to sewing to earn money. Sewing is a traditional household skill practiced essentially by all Chilean women, who often out of necessity make most of the clothes for their families as well as articles for the home.

It is easy now to ask with hindsight, "How was it possible to form an organization of such power when all legal means of organizing seemed totally blocked?" But the fact is they did not have any overall grand strategy when they began; they simply set to work to try to meet the most pressing needs of their parishoners, and the Committee expanded as the needs grew. The Pro-Paz Committee was without precedent in the religious, political and social history of Chile. The priests, feeling helpless at not knowing what had happened to so many members of their parishes, united, cooperated and constructed this unusual committee that accomplished a tremendous amount of work during the two years it was allowed to operate. Records show that approximately fifty-four people sought their aid each day. Their main task was to provide basic support of all types for bereft families including legal aid in cases of detained-disappeared. They made heroic efforts on behalf of the *disappeared*, working with families all over Chile. Their main base of operations, however, was in Santiago.

It was in this context that the arpilleristas emerged. They were mostly housewives living in the shantytowns. Some washed clothes or did other marginal and menial work to earn a little money; many had never worked outside the home before. They got to know each other as they inquired in prisons, police stations, detention centres for their family members who had been detained, or they met in places where they went to ask for aid because their husbands were out of work. It was through families left behind and destitute that the Pro-Paz Committee and the Catholic Church (and later the outside world) became aware of the extent and severity of the repression in Chile, and it was from the testimonies made to the Committee by families of the missing that the Committee was able to compile the first statistics on the *disappeared*. By the end of September, 1973 (remember that the coup occurred on the 11th) the Committee had received notice of 3000 cases of disappearances, and four-hundred people on the average were arrested each month in the first months following the coup.[5] It has recently been estimated by Amnesty International that as many as 90,000 people in Latin America have disappeared under various dictatorships during the last ten-fifteen years.

One of the many programs started by the Pro-Paz Committee was a network of medical clinics to care for malnourished children, and a nationwide child-feeding program. Out of the participants of this group came the organization known as the Association of the Detained-Disappeared. The first twenty members of the Association were arpilleristas, whose workshop served as a model for all subsequent ones. By 1973 there were seventy-five members of the Association; at the present time the membership is about four hundred, and of these, forty women are active in the arpillera workshops as well.

The Pro-Paz Committee received financial aid from a variety of international organizations, most particularly from the World

Council of Churches that contributed some $1,800,000 to its support. In 1975 the Committee was forced to dismantle under pressure from the government of General Pinochet, who in one of the messages sent to Cardinal Silva Henríquez, said: "For various reasons we consider that the above mentioned organization is a medium used by the Marxists-Leninists to create problems that disturb the tranquillity of the people and the necessary peace of the country, the maintenance of which is the principal duty of the government.... We would view then the dissolving of the Committee in question as a positive step toward avoiding worse evils."[6]

Once the Pro-Paz Committee was dissolved, Cardinal Silva Henríquez wasted no time in forming another one. The next month he set up an organization that could not be dissolved because it functions entirely within the strict ecumenical laws of the Catholic Church and the office of the Archbishop. Naturally the new organization is also subject to internal tensions, since as we pointed out earlier, Church officials differ in their political opinions as does the rest of the population. Some prelates still believe that political problems of the country can be solved by means of a courteous exchange of letters between officials and through polite, private conversations.[7].

So essentially as soon as the Pro-Paz Committee closed its doors, the Vicarate of Solidarity (Vicaría de la Solidaridad) opened for business, as an integral part of the office of the Archbishop of Santiago, the only way for such an organization to exist and operate beyond the reach of the fascist dictatorship. Very quickly the Vicarate established twenty regional offices in different areas of the country that began to offer legal aid, health care and work opportunities. More than 700,000 people were aided in the first months. The arpillera workshops were also taken under the protective wing of the Vicarate.

In 1979 the Vicarate was feeding meals to almost 5,000,000 people. Among their other activities, they began to publish a bi-weekly newspaper, *Solidaridad,* which listed services available at their centres, and also gave news of police sweeps and arrests that had taken place in the poor neighbourhoods and shantytowns.

There was a rash of such sweeps in May of 1986—The Boston *Globe* of May 10 reported eight raids in eleven days. The newly named Archbishop of Santiago, Juan Francisco Fresno, strongly condemned the mass detentions and demanded that the government of Pinochet stop using troops in the slum communities. (Air Force paratroopers were conducting the searches). However, Archbishop Fresno's attempt to influence Pinochet was entirely without effect. The sweeps and mass detentions continue. These constant attacks, then and now, only serve to strengthen the resolve of the Church to continue its efforts. Another result has been that many people who had drifted away from the Church have been attracted back. These include many intellectuals of liberal political leanings. Obviously the Vicarate from its earliest days has been under heavy attack by the government of Pinochet and the attacks have been aimed above all at the arpilleristas, a point we will come back to later on. But since the Vicarate is set up as an ecumenical body of the Church it has been able to survive the attacks mounted against it, and to maintain a very strong position in spite of the various means used against it by the Government. Instead, its position as an independent group working in opposition to the fascist government has been fortified. The Pinochet government began to take action against some Catholic schools, banning certain texts considered dangerous for the education of the youth of Chile, and to dictate what could be taught in universities, most particularly the Catholic University. In other areas the Government could not interfere directly with the "policies" and activities of the Vicarate that were considered religious and charitable in nature, areas traditionally proper for the attention of the Church, but there is no doubt that the autonomy of the Vicarate was guaranteed more by its international support and visibility than by the desire of the Government to act in a correct and legally proper manner toward the Church. The Junta showed no hesitation in interfering with instruction and activities at the religious colleges that are supported by Government funds, and so in a subject position.

The programs of the Vicarate of Solidarity to aid the unemployed, the workshops, and other activities followed the pattern set earlier by its precursor, the Pro-Paz Committee. The concepts as well as the organizational structure were more or less taken over intact. Concerning the workshop program in particular, Pro-Paz and the Vicarate made a tremendous effort to provide work for the indigent. The Vicarate set up not only arpillera workshops in Santiago, but other types of craft shops throughout the country. They established workshops for political prisoners in internal exile on Dawson Island and in other jails where political prisoners produced artisanry items worked in copper and bone.

It is difficult to find direct information about the prison workshops, but it is known that no special space was set aside for them. In the summer prisoners worked in patios of the prison and in in the winter in their cells. As in the case of all the artisans and the arpilleristas, the Vicarate provided the materials, bought the finished articles from the workers, usually a monthly quota, and the money received by the members of each group was divided equally among them. The Vicarate then undertook to sell the work, mostly abroad, and money from sales was used to purchase more materials. As we shall see in more detail later, the arpilleras made in Santiago became very well known for their political themes. There was another workshop that also produced crafts of a political type — small dolls made of wool yarn popularly known throughout the country as "Black José". The dolls have no arms and no legs and were immediately adopted as a symbol of a maimed and impotent country.[8]

However it is the arpilleras from the Vicarate workshops that provide the most damning and accurate picture of the political climate of the county. As a craft, arpilleras are not unique to Chile. They are made in Peru and Colombia, for example, but as of now, the arpilleras made in Santiago are the only ones to have political themes. Here it is interesting to note that artisans in Nicaragua have begun to use the appliqué technique of the Chilean arpilleras to create scenes of the new Nicaragua: cheerful scenes of schools and hospitals, very different indeed from the scenes of the Chilean arpilleras. What we might call the political arpillera has developed only in the poor neighbourhoods ringing Santiago. Women from other parts of the country, particularly women from the rural areas have continued to work within a more traditional framework, creating flowers and fields, children playing, fiestas, peaceful pastures. We will come back to this point later when we discuss the Bordadoras de Isla Negra (The Embroiderers of Isla Negra).

The first arpillera workshop to be formed was composed of members of the Association of the Detained-Disappeared in 1974 in order to provide immediate aid to families psychologically and economically devastated by the disappearance of their loved ones. No one thought then that throughout long years these workshops would provide the main means of survival for many women. Now the women worry about the commercialization of their arpilleras, about overproduction, and a decline in the number of buyers. I have found an interesting point of view as I have travelled around to numerous universities in the United States showing the arpilleras and talking about them. It appears that it is difficult for many people, at least in the United States, to understand that the arpilleras are not just another consumer product that could be marketed according to the newest techniques.[9] The arpilleras of Santiago are not made in hopes of huge sales and a tremendous income. They can't be sent through the mail easily or shipped in great crates by freighter or air cargo. The Junta does not want them to leave the country. And then each arpillera is totally hand made by one woman, and it takes about a week to finish one, provided the maker is able to work on it regularly. But the women who make them have heavy responsibilities and other obligations. They are in no sense of the word "piece workers" on an assembly line. The arpilleras do bring in some very needed income to their creators, but they are, above all, a way of expressing what is in the heart and soul, things that are too painful or impossible to say in words, and they are an attempt to show what has happened in Chile and to awaken the conscience of the country and the outside world. The arpilleras are born of the necessity to survive, and remain a clandestine art. Due to the harassment and constant vigilance of the government of Pinochet, the arpilleras have to be sent abroad in small groups in an attempt to avoid detection. Those found in the luggage of travellers at airports, for instance, are seized. It is forbidden to show, much less sell, the arpilleras inside Chile.

We have not been able to determine the exact origins of the Santiago arpilleras.[10] The tradition of using left-over scraps of material to make new material, out of which practical or decorative articles can be constructed — quilts, patch-work of all sorts, jackets and skirts — is very old and widespread. Within the area of Chilean popular art the nearest form to the Santiago arpilleras are the tapestries made by Violeta Parra in the 1950s. Violeta Parra was a folklorist, most known for her songs which she composed herself and sang all over Chile. But she was an artist who was inspired by the folk tradition and revived it in the areas of music, visual arts and crafts, and fiestas. She spoke for the poor and oppressed and became a symbol, especially for the young and the compassionate part of the population, and was an inspiration for artists of all persuasions. She committed suicide in 1967. Both Violeta's tapestries and the Santiago arpilleras used very simple material such as feed sacks as a backing cloth (*arpillera* in Spanish means simply burlap — hence the name); however Violeta's arpilleras reflected scenes of daily life, Chilean folklore and festivals, since part of her purpose was to revive and preserve all forms of popular art and to make them meaningful for new generations. But she was first and foremost an artist, and very well-known by the time she was making her arpilleras. Her creations might be regarded as another one of her artistic experiments, using simple found objects and pieces, scraps and fragments of wool yarn. She exhibited and sold her arpilleras at craft fairs in and around Santiago for very modest prices. Now they are highly prized as art and very high priced, both rightly so, since they represent a vital cross between Chilean popular art and fine art. We believe the same might happen in the future with the Santiago arpilleras — that they will be held in as high regard as Violeta's, since they will provide a most vivid, revealing chronicle of life in Chile under Pinochet.

Another possible inspiration for the Santiago arpilleras might be the embroideries of Isla Negra. Beginning in the 1960s, women, mostly wives of fishermen and farmers in the little fishing port of Isla

Negra, 120 km. southwest of Santiago, and long time home of Pablo Neruda, began using colourful wool yarn to embroider local scenes: the harvest, threshing the grain, fishermen at sea. This particular type of embroidery has no clear antecedent in Chilean crafts; it only goes back about twenty years and was fostered by Doña Leonor Sobrino de Vera, who is a long time resident of Isla Negra and wanted to do something to help the families who had only fish or crops to depend on for income. The bordados (embroideries) and the role of Doña Leonor are discussed in detail in Chapter IV. Here we might just say that the Isla Negra embroideries represent an artistic leap from the traditional needlework practiced by women all over the country. Another artistic legacy of Chilean woollen crafts made by women are the beautiful ponchos made in the village of Doñihue, about one hour's drive from Santiago. The designs are traditional Araucanian Indian designs woven in red against a gray background.

Many people are familiar with the *molas* made by the Cuna Indians of the San Blas Islands of Panama. These are small wall hangings, the designs a colourful mix showing mythical, imaginary and real animals, birds and flowers of the Islands. The *molas* look similar to appliqué, but the technique is more complex. It consists of sewing together several layers of cloth, each of a different colour, then cutting through different thicknesses to reveal the design. All of these crafts may have had an influence on the arpilleras of Santiago. No matter their origin, the arpilleras of Santiago are something new.

As mentioned earlier the first arpillera workshop was formed by members of the Association of the Detained-Disappeared, and from the first seemed equally important as a way for the women to get together and share their griefs and sorrows as it was a way to earn money. Later with aid from the Vicarate of Solidarity the workshops began to proliferate. They were established in different zones which were called Centro, Norte, Oeste, Oriente, Sur, Rural y Costa (Centre, North, West, East, South, Rural and Coast). All workshops were organized in the same way: they received material from the Vicarate and depended on the Vicarate for the sale of the work.

However, as time went on and the women gained more experience, they began to operate with more autonomy. They sought outlets on their own, conducted their own business, and the Vicarate acted more in a consultant capacity than as a managerial body. Some women raffled off arpilleras in their neighbourhoods; they told me they thought in those early days that only their friends would buy the arpilleras.

Operation, Staffing and Training of the Workshops

The workshops fix a date once a month for the finished arpilleras to be turned in. The elected treasurer of the group takes them herself to the Vicarate which buys them. The number bought each month varies according to money on hand and the number of arpilleras coming in, but the rule of thumb is, each woman makes four arpilleras a month (one a week). Most of the material for the arpilleras, provided by the Vicarate, is collected by them through appeals within Chile and abroad. New material is handed out to each group as the batches of finished arpilleras are brought in. Again it should be pointed out that the amount of material on hand at any one time is variable, subject to chance, luck, or streaks of scarcity. The making of the arpilleras remains a shoestring operation.

Technical assistance for making the first arpilleras was provided by volunteers trained in the plastic arts, women like Valentina Bonne, a painter. (See her testimony in Chapter V). According to accounts of the women, they were told at first to make scenes of their daily life, the things they saw and to express what they felt. They began by cutting out little figures, but they were flat, lifeless and without movement. Their first houses were all similar and made of gray cloth. The women themselves say they never thought anyone was going to buy what they were making; that they were ugly and that nobody would be interested in the lives of poor people.

After this first stage, however, the women learned to observe more carefully, and it was as though in trying to see their own modest surroundings with more clarity, they were led to a clearer

51

vision of what was happening in the country. "I walked around like an idiot," one woman told me. "I looked closely at everything. I believe I learned how to see." Another said, "The first arpilleras were very hard to make. It was so difficult, that blanket stitch that we were making. It is the same stitch that we use now to make the edging. Later they taught us the cross stitch and that was much easier." The perception that the arpilleristas themselves had of their early work is interesting, because their views were to change as years went on and they became more skilled and more self-confident. But more than that, the arpillera ceased to be just a means of earning their daily bread and became an outlet for their feelings, a method of social, artistic, metaphorical, and political expression. One woman, still speaking of the early days, said, "It was hard. We would come to the meetings because we had to work together and the men at home didn't want us to go out. But I had to earn some money so we could eat. Later I began to enjoy the work because we were learning new things."

This "learning new things" is a very important outcome of the arpillera workshops. The arpilleristas — housewives, seamstresses, laundresses — assumed a new identity that added an important dimension to their traditional female role. Now they were no longer totally tied to domestic chores in their own homes. The workshop made the women part of a group outside home and family where they could discuss common problems, or indeed anything they wanted, earn money of their own, many for the first time in their lives, and get involved in the political realities of their life and their country. These realities began to be expressed with truth and fidelity in the arpilleras.

"We gathered in the dining room to discuss ways to beat off hunger and one woman thought of making little dolls of white cloth. It didn't make sense, then we began to add little flowers, and they came out better, but nobody bought them, they were so ugly." However, after the first exhibition and sale of arpilleras in San Ignacio's School (when it was still possible to sell the arpilleras in Chile) the women had a new sense of purpose in life and a feeling of greater security. One woman expressed it this way: "Before I never talked with anyone and I was used to the fact that my husband beat me and I never did anything to defend myself. But afterwards I learned to have friends and to speak up in the meetings."

"The beginning was hard," said another woman. "The dolls seemed so lifeless on the surface of the arpillera until one woman thought of making them as rounded little figures with clothes and all. So the little people turned out to be active, lively, versatile."

The first step for each arpillerista is to decide on the theme of what she wants to portray, and after her idea is discussed with the group, the shapes that form the background are cut: the Andes (always the Andes), a sun, clouds, rooftoops. One by one the elements are sewn in place. That's the way the arpillera is constructed: the scene is set, and within the scene as in a stage set, the action, the drama is created by adding the dolls and other elements.

Making the main characters of the scene is the most difficult part — they have to tell the story. The heads of the dolls are made separately. Small squares of cloth are cut, filled with bits of fabric and sewed together. Knots are carefully hidden at the neck of the doll, or covered by hair. The hair is usually made of black yarn, but if no proper yarn is available, women use locks from their own hair. The eyes and mouth are formed by small embroidery stitches. Then come the clothes. The skirts are small squares gathered at the top so they will flare at the bottom, pants are formed of two small rectangles. The clothes are made of all different kinds of patterned material giving a more real and lifelike appearance to the scene. When the doll is dressed head to foot it is attached to the arpillera in the proper place. Other three-dimensional elements are often added: small twigs for fire wood (red embroidery stitches create the flames); matchsticks or toothpicks make the clubs the police carry to beat people; tin foil creates the shiny metallic helments the police wear; tiny articles of clothing hang on an embroidered laundry line. So the arpillera comes to life under the hands of its creator; more than that, it *is* the life of the creator, since the dolls often wear clothes made from her own clothes and sometimes, as we said earlier, hair from her own head.

The staffing of the workshops changed as time went on. The more experienced women taught the newer members; they all helped each other with difficult problems; they went through their apprenticeship together. They were learning not only sewing techniques, but learning to look, to see, to transform what they saw and felt into pictures, how to manage their affairs, and to get along in a group.

Although the arpillera workshops became more autonomous, the relationship between the Vicarate and the various groups was always one of warm friendliness, concern and mutual respect, as it still is today. Themes were never imposed on the groups by the Vicarate. An arpillerista from the Oriente Zone explained, "We don't accept the imposition of any themes for our arpilleras, naturally there were problems. For our own safety they (the Vicarate) didn't want us to denounce what was happening. In some workshops the women were more docile, but in the end our point of view won out." But let us emphasize that this attempt on the part of the Vicarate to ban political denunciation as a theme for the arpilleras was only to try to protect the lives of the women themselves, many of whom had been arrested more than once in their homes and held for varying periods of time in prison. In recent years the harassment of all those connected with the arpillera workshops has grown worse and even staff members of the Vicarate have been threatened. Manuel Parada, one of the Vicarate's volunteer lawyers working on cases involving violation of human rights, was brutally murdered in 1984 by having his throat cut. But in spite of all that, the Vicarate has stood firm and the profound solidarity and respect linking the Vicarate and the arpillera workshops is still strong and intact.

The formation of the workshops and their manner of operating always veered toward a communal effort, and it is now possible to see the historical leading role played by the women as a result of joining with other women to discuss and try to resolve common problems. There is no doubt that the arpilleras, the vision of the world as seen by these women will be one of the most important testimonies left of this dark epoch of Chilean history.

CEMA CHILE or Artisanry as Official Discourse

Up to now we have been describing how workshops arose as a result of the efforts of organizations formed especially to provide some protection for the victims of Pinochet's repressive policies. We should point out that when the Christian Democrats were in power (1967-1970) an organization called CEMA CHILE (Centros de Madres para Artesanía) was set up for the purpose of giving courses and training in crafts to poor women from marginal neighbourhoods of the city. Classes were offered in weaving, ceramics, knitting and other needlework. At the time of its founding CEMA was totally non-political, but as is natural, it did become somewhat politicized as time went on. Under Pinochet, however, CEMA CHILE has been taken over for outright political purposes. (All the information on CEMA has been taken from Lechner and Levy, Footnote 12). CEMA CHILE is directed by Pinochet's wife, Lucía Hiriarte de Pinochet, and under her leadership all the stereotypes of women's place in society are heavily reinforced, with obsessive interest being placed on women's duty to serve the Fatherland and the Father of the Country, who is, of course, Pinochet. [12]

It goes without saying that the organization and management of CEMA CHILE differs radically from the Vicarate workshops. A member of CEMA explained very frankly: "The centres of CEMA CHILE have a vertical organizational structure and direction that comes from above, straight from the Government by way of women volunteers gathered together under the National Department of Women's Affairs,"[13] which was instituted on October 17, 1973,[14] only a month and six days after the coup. The idea was for Pinochet to try to hold onto — and to manipulate — the support he had received from many middle and upper-class women. It was really an anti-Allende movement, and there is no doubt that it helped bring Pinochet to power. These were women who feared losing their easy life and privileged positions under a more egalitarian, Socialist regime. As Lechner and Levy say: "(The Department of Women's Affairs) is not meant for women, but is rather a women's organization created to serve the patriarchy." Among its statutes they emphasize the following stated aims: "To disseminate values of the country and family, to create in women a national conscience and a correct understanding of the dignity and importance of their mis ion; (2) To promote and channel women's support of the gov rnment, giving them the opportunity to serve as volunteers and to offer their cooperation in programs of development that the Government promotes."[15] Note that no direct economic aid is available to women through the Department of Women's Affairs.

A member of a CEMA workshop made this illuminating statement: "If you're all alone with your problems it's worse....You have to put up with everything, being poor, unemployed, a husband that drinks, kids who are hungry, then with all that on your shoulders, you have to get out, leave the kids and look for some money . . . and most of the time you don't find it even by screaming your head off."[16] The mood of this statement is in sharp contrast to the feeling of energy and solidarity expressed by women in the Vicarate workshops.

As we have already observed, from the earliest days of its takeover by the Pinochet regime, CEMA was in effect a doctrinaire, propagandistic, political entity. Its director, however, Señora Lucía (Pinochet) describes the purpose in another fashion. "I decided to intervene in a definitive fashion to save and develop our native art."[17] CEMA uses its members in different ways. Volunteer committee members as well as women from the workshops swell the audiences at talks and lectures designed obviously to bring out the patriotic spirit of women and convince them of their duty to serve the country as mothers and obedient wives. The spirit of liberation hardly exists in Pinochet's Chile. These gatherings also afford a friendly forum for Pinochet's speeches.

CEMA, in line with its announced intention to foster native crafts, has organized workshops in different sections of the city where groups of women, about twenty in each group, meet to work under the direction of a monitor. It is not possible to find out exactly what happens on a day-to-day basis in the workshops because their activities are kept strictly secret. One feels an atmosphere of suspicion and distrust hovering around the workshops. The members are said to consider people on the outside as *enemies*, which creates a great gap between those inside and those outside. In addition the women in the CEMA groups are forbidden to talk about what they do with outsiders. The centres are then a mini-version of the authoritarian regime of Pinochet.

We have learned that all decisions are made at the top and instructions for implementing them are handed down to the women who do the work. Themes are assigned; there is no discussion among the workers. The old assembly-line mentality seems to be the ruling dynamic: that as much work as possible be done in the shortest possible time. The lack of any possibility for a creative spirit to develop is at considerable variance with the official publicity put out by CEMA, which portrays itself as a big harmonious family. One such statement reads, in part: "Ustedes dejaron de ser persona ya son pertenecientes a una institución y están bajo el cuidado de esa gran gallina llamada CEMA CHILE." Anyone reading that statement, and trying to translate it, has to ponder carefully what might be the meaning(s) of the *persona*: it can mean they have stopped being persons, individuals, and can also mean, in Chilean usage, that they have stopped being persons alone. Here is a possible translation: "You are no longer persons (alone) now that you belong to an institution under the care of this great mother hen called CEMA CHILE."[18]

This is typical of the official CEMA rhetoric that constantly refers to the matriarchal, sheltering nature of the organization, the mother hen protecting her baby chicks under her wings. It is ironic that CEMA, supposed to be for the benefit and betterment of women, is very clearly based on an ideology that reinforces the old roles of women, as a domestic being only, and constantly repeats the political indoctrination that women must stay the same as always: weak and dependent.

CEMA maintains a strict vigilance over the different centres and particularly over the control of the *carnets* — identification cards issued to the women who have been accepted into the workshops after a probation period of about six months. This *carnet* entitles the holder to important benefits, such as the right to shop at discount prices at CEMA-owned grocery stores and other businesses, and to receive health care at CEMA-run health clinics. Obviously these are tremendously valuable assets for many women who are in serious economic difficulties. Many join the CEMA workshops because of the benefits and because the workshops have the reputation of being an efficient way to make some money. However, the women in the Vicarate workshops, who are on the whole in much greater need and who suffer so severely from the disappearances of family members as well as loss of livelihood, say they would never join a CEMA group. Even if they tried to join, it is very unlikely they would be admitted. Since the Vicarate workshops are closely surveilled, the identities of the women are presumably all known. And the other way around, if a woman from a CEMA workshop defected to a Vicarate workshop, or even if she simply left the CEMA workshop, she would immediately lose her *carnet*, and all the privileges that go with it, and more than that, expose herself to serious physical abuse as well. There are stories of women who left CEMA and who have been roughed up and beaten by goon squads. There is also a rumour that one woman was tortured personally by Pinochet's wife for deserting CEMA. We were, of course, not able to substantiate these stories and rumours, but the fact is, that true or not, they are believed.

It is clear that CEMA CHILE operates as an integral part of the Pinochet regime, with the workshops and their members being under the direct control of official government administrators. The women who make up the administration of CEMA present themselves as symbols of the country. But their idea of country goes back to a paternalism that in turn is based on feudalism. Vestiges of this feudal/paternalistic past still exist in many countries, including Chile, that are still economically underdeveloped and where a great difference in social classes still exists. Well-to-do-women of the upper classes, for complex reasons — tradition, to salve their consciences, to have something to do, because harmless charitable activities are one of the few outlets for action allowed them — play Lady Bountiful to women of the poor and lower classes. They provide yarn or cloth, teach the poor women in their "care" to knit, or sew, or make little things. CEMA CHILE is following exactly in this pattern. The traditional pattern of helping the poor, through an official organ of the government like CEMA, was widened and modified considerably during the government of Eduardo Frei and the Christian Democrats (1967-71). They made a concerted effort to make the society more open and more democratic on all fronts.

After Frei's Christian Democratic party lost to Allende in 1971, the role of CEMA changed again under the Allende Socialist regime. By looking at CEMA and its various metamorphoses over the decades, it is possible to see the intricate interweaving of women, politics and society. To give a brief history of CEMA and the direct involvement of governments in women's affairs, we have to go back to the very original precursor of the Mothers' Centres, or CEMA, begun in 1954, when the so-called Ropero del Pueblo (Clothes for the People) was created.[19] Ropero del Pueblo was a private, charitable foundation to aid the poor. From it came in 1962 the idea of aiding women in an official way, and to this end the Department of Women's Affairs of the Christian Democrats formally founded CEMA which was still based on the concept of Christian charity and of helping one's neighbours. Centres were set up and the idea behind them was to attempt to develop local leadership for each group, and to foster self-help projects, since each neighbourhood had different problems. During the time of the United Popular Front (1970-73), CEMA continued to operate basically according to the pattern established by and inherited from the Christian Democrats, but Allende's government widened the scope of the centres and incorporated them with other services all placed near one another in Neighbourhood Centres. Thus CEMA came to have a double organization: the overall administrative group called COCEMA, The National Confederation of Mothers' Centres, undertook to teach members how to organize on a community level to solve basic problems. The Social Assistance, or welfare, offices, health centres and clinics, child-care centres were all clustered in locations in each neighbourhood. Neighbourhood groups working on specific problems were also placed near these clusters. The idea was to promote a small, autonomous, local government for each neighbourhood. These reforms were very important and represented a real advance for women who were accepted in the neighbourhood organizations and played leading roles. However, COSEMA and all the other centres ceased to exist the day Pinochet took over. Against this backdrop we can appreciate the calamitous situation the poor, especially poor women, found themselves in immediately after the coup. They were thrown into extreme anguish and misery and their entire support system collapsed.

The "new" ideology of CEMA, imposed when the organization was brought back to life by the military government in October, 1975, is really the "oldest" ideology. It is an enormous backward step as far as the advancement of women in Chile is concerned. The women of CEMA are manipulated as just one more pawn in the process of reconstructing the country, top to bottom, according to Pinochet's ideal. What Pinochet wants is what his wife wants and now what CEMA wants. What one says the other parrots. Under the two previous regimes, CEMA was beginning to decentralize and allow the local groups more autonomy. Now it is an organization of masses. Women are useful objects to be manipulated, to be turned out for rallies and manifestations that support the government, and beneath it all runs the ideological thread that proclaims women's only destiny is the traditional one as self-sacrificing producer of sons for the glory of the Fatherland. A member of CEMA today is required to submit to the mandates of those in power and to conform in every way to traditional social discipline.

Finally, to close this section on the official artisanry produced by CEMA CHILE workshops, I would like to quote the following instructions given to a group by the monitor-leader to those responsible for admitting new members. "Be careful with the people you receive (into the group) . . . don't take in immediately just any group that arrives without knowing who they are and why they want to enter the Centre . . . . Only after six months will a *carnet* be issued to the new member and the social worker does not provide any help for a new (probationary) member who does not have a *carnet* and who does not yet appear on the official list of new members."[20]

It is very understandable that women of few economic

resources, who may very well not be in political agreement with CEMA, i.e., the Pinochet regime, feel obliged to join it for the benefits they can derive from it. CEMA dampens their hunger pangs and in return gains a very efficient way to control and exploit the poor. In this manner CEMA controls the lives of significant numbers of the poor of the population. Within the dialectic of utilitarianism is found a cynicism displaying a false picture of a country governed by those who care for the people and are dedicated to order and peace.

THE ARPILLERAS OF THE VICARATE WORKSHOPS AND GOVERNMENT POLICY TOWARD THEM

It would seem that the arpilleras of the Vicarate workshops, never made in any great quantity, would not amount to enough to arouse the wrath of the official press in Chile. However, exactly the opposite is the case. CEMA CHILE, some of whose members occasionally infiltrate the Vicarate workshops, on orders from above, obviously, considering facts discussed in the previous section, constantly denounce the work of the Vicarate arpilleristas in the press. The Vicarate workshops have no CEMA-type system to protect themselves from such infiltration, and we don't need to point out that the press, including newspapers, radio and television, magazines, books, book and magazine sellers, all operate under fierce censorship restrictions. In addition, the offices and workshops of the Vicarate are under constant surveillance, much of it by hidden camera. With all this, we must conclude that each arpillera, successfully completed and sent out of the country, is a victory and a miracle, as is each day that the arpilleristas are able to stay free and work.

During my research I collected a number of articles from newspapers in Santiago attacking the Vicarate arpilleristas. The clippings came from *El Mercurio*, the major daily newspaper in Santiago, from *La Segunda, La Tercera*, and others.[21] The rhetoric was obvious and always the same: that the only aim of the arpilleristas was to defame the government; that the Vicarate is an opposition political group full of Marxist and "foreign" priests. Here are some typical headlines:

"NEEDLECRAFTS MEANT TO OPPOSE THE GOVERNMENT"

"SCRAPS OF LIFE — Who Exports These Scraps of Life?"

"SENDING OF SUBVERSIVE MATERIAL ABROAD DISCOVERED"

"NOT JUST AN ARPILLERA"

"SHIPMENT OF SUBVERSIVE PROPAGANDA DISCOVERED BY CUSTOMS . . ."

"THE SENDING ABROAD OF INFAMOUS WALL HANGINGS CONTINUES"

and the list goes on and on, day after day, up to the present time.

It is revealing to quote from one particular article and to note the attempt to smear the arpilleras, the women who make them, as well as the Vicarate that sponsors them. The headline reads: "DISRESPECT FOR WOMEN" and the article, unsigned, which is usual in these cases, goes on to say: "One of the tapestries that we show here (in a photograph of a faked arpillera — Author's note) represents a father who asks his daughters to help him procure some money. The only way they can think of to help him is to work as prostitutes. So they search for male companions and go to a hotel. Soon after they come back to their home and hand over the money they have earned to their father. This idea is only one of the infamies that the Vicarate fosters against the national honour. This time we have an obligation to denounce not only the danger such actions represent for Chile but for Chilean womanhood also." This language is very similar to that used by CEMA CHILE in one of their booklets as we can see by the following paragraph: "Everybody knows the determination of the women of our country and the untiring fight they wage against Marxism. Everybody remembers how they marched with their empty pots and their constant battles to liberate the country from Marxism, and now to say that their only recourse is to prostitute themselves is an infamy." But back to the newspaper article quoted from above, it goes on to say, "Does a tapestry

62

showing Chilean women as prostitutes really help Chilean women? Can it be true that the women of our country, untiring fighters for the welfare of their households and for the good of the Fatherland, can find no other solution for her difficulties than to become prostitutes?"

Note that in these quotes the major role of the women is made out to be not that of prostitute or sexual object, but that of servant of the Nation. But the word *prostitute* in various forms is repeated over and over throughout this extensive article to the extent that it will remain in the ear of the hasty or unaware reader. Let us add here, as a postscript to the propaganda quoted above, that the number of prostitutes has gone up in Chile by 50 percent since 1973, and that is due entirely to the economic misery of the country.

We have been able to observe throughout this study that women's lives are intimately and inextricably tied to the political events of the country, either because they get involved of their own free will or because they are manipulated into helping one faction or another as is happening now under the Pinochet regime. Consider for instance another newspaper article, said to be written by women members of an organization known by the initials of AMA, Asociación Mundial Antimarxista (World Anti-marxist Association). It appeared in the newspaper, *La Tercera*, on July 17, 1977, p. 24. It goes like this:

"NOT JUST AN ARPILLERA"

"It's not just arpilleras that are spreading calumny and infamy. Well-known priests and other religious workers of Chile, with the support and protection of the Holy Cape, have allowed themselves to become involved in the dissemination of public documents which are critical of the strictly political problems of the country. The high religious function is twisted by foreign and national clerics who, in their office in the Plaza de Armas, cover the walls with grotesque embroideries as a symbol of their revolutionary pastoral duties. Who can stop the demagoguery that these priests foment from their command headquarters of the Vicarate of Solidarity?"

This attack is proof of the fact that the government has not been able to stop the "demogoguery" and the scraps of life keep right on chronicling the stories of death in the Chile of Pinochet. The creation of the arpillera in Chile demonstrates that in spite of the fact that the government is obsessed by the culture of death, the women in the Vicarate workshops keep on saying *Yes* to life.

FOOTNOTES

1 A large part of the information in this chapter comes from internal documents of the Vicarate of Solidarity, especially publications for the years 1974-75. We have also used, as general background information, the book of Hernán Vidal, *Dar la vida por la vida* (Give Life for Life). Minneapolis: Institute for the Study of Ideologies and Literature, 1982. It is a vital source for the history of the Detained-Disappeared.

2 This information comes directly from the only document of the Pro-Paz Committee, also for internal circulation, made available to me by the Department of Publications of the Vicarate under the title: *Cooperación para la paz en Chile, Crónica de sus dos años de labor solidaria, 1973-1975.* Santiago: Vicaría de la Solidaridad, 1975.

3 Document from the Pro-Paz Committee, Introduction. No page number.

4 The basic book concerning the Church in Chile is by Brian Smith, *The Church and Politics in Chile*. Princeton: Princeton University Press, 1982. In addition we would like to mention the interesting study by Virginia Marie Bouvier, *Alliance or Compliance: Implications of the Chilean Experience for the Catholic Church in Latin America.* Syracuse: Maxwell School of Citizenship and Public Affairs, Syracuse University, 1983. Those interested in studying in more detail the relationship between women and the Church in Chile should see the article by Katherine Gilfeather, Women Religious, The Poor and the Institutional Church in Chile. *Journal of Interamerican Studies* and World Affairs 21. (Feb. 1979) pp. 125-55.

5 Information from Pro-Paz Committee. Internal document. No page number.

6 Ibid.

7 Brian Smith, *The Church and Politics in Chile,* p. 299.

8 The information for this section comes from my personal experience and many interviews and conversations, and also from the book by Cecilia Moreno Aliste, *La artesanía urbana marginal* (Artisanry of the Urban Marginal Communities). Santiago: Ceneca, July, 1984.
I have relied most heavily on Chapter II, dedicated to the arpilleras.

9 See for example the article in *Newsweek Magazine* on the Peruvian arpilleras. "Sunrise in the Slums," June 24, 1985, p. 64.

10 For more information on artisanry in Chile see Tomás Logo, *Artesanía popular chilena* (Popular Crafts of Chile). Santiago: Editorial Universitario, 1974. For a general study of the subject see the book *Folk Arts of the Americas,* edited by August Panijella. New York: Harry N. Abrams, 1981.

11 Internal document of the Vicarate called *Arpilleras.* Edited by Manuel Paiva and is based on testimonies of arpilleristas.

12 Information for this section is based on the following document: *Notas sobre la vida cotidiana: el disciplinamiento de la mujer* (Notes on Daily Life: The Disciplining of Women), by Norberto Lechner and Susana Levy. Flacso (Facultad Latinoamericana de Ciencias Sociales), No. 57, July, 1984. Santiago.

13 Lechner and Levy, p. 32.

14 Ibid. pp. 52-3.

15 Ibid. p. 57.

16 Ibid. p. 45.

17 Ibid. p. 52.

18 Ibid. p. 62.

19 For information concerning el Ropero del Pueblo (Clothes for the People) see the book by Felicitas Klimpel, *La mujer chilena: El aporte femenino al progreso de Chile* (The Chilean Woman: Women's Support for the Progress of Chile). Santiago: Andrés Bello, 1962, p. 62.

20 Lechner and Levy, p 50.

21 This information has been compiled from various daily newspapers of Santiago between 1974 and 1983. I have collected about forty articles from *Las Ultimas Noticias, La Tercera,* and *El Mercurio,* among others. All quotes from newspaper articles come from this collection.

CHAPTER 4

IN THE WORKSHOPS

My first hand knowledge of the arpillera workshops dates from the end of December, 1979. At first I was always accompanied to the meetings by a supervisor from the Vicarate of Solidarity. Later, however, I was able to make contacts on my own with a number of the arpilleristas and gradually become friends with some of them. It was not easy to enter their world. Little by little I had to gain their respect and confidence, convince them that I was genuinely interested in their welfare, and only wanted to *listen* to them so that I could re-tell their stories, this story, to the outside world.

I never pretended to be purely objective in my dealings with the women in the workshops. I came to them commited to their cause, simply wanting to know more about them. Slowly they accepted me, took me in as part of their lives. I shared their pain, the bad moments when the work would be interrupted by sobs. In this chapter I attempt to give my very personal impressions of the time I spent in the workshops, and wherever possible, I let the women speak for themselves.

The workshops are scattered throughout different areas of the city, in churches, in or near the neighbourhoods where most of the women live. In general, the churches in these marginal neighbour-hoods are themselves extremely modest. Usually the workshop would be located in whatever space was available, at the end of a long, dimly lit corridor, or in basements. The regular meetings of the members vary according to each workshop: some meet once a week,

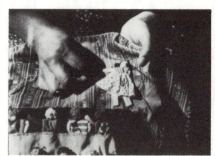

as she tenderly
picks through the remnants of her dead,
salvages the shroud of her husband
the trousers left after the absences

she conjures up victorious armies
embroiders humble people smiling, become triumphant
brings the dead back to life

from *The Arpillerista* by Marjorie Agosin

others ev ᵣy fifteen days. Most of the work on the arpilleras takes place at home. The most serious practical problem the women have is lack of adequate lighting when they work. Making arpilleras is extra work done for extra income, and therefore done whenever extra time can be found, either in the evenings or in the early mornings before the regular chores begin, times when there is little or no natural light. Many of the houses have no electricity because the people have been unable to pay their bills and their service has been cut off. For the most part their houses have no heat either, and the evenings and early mornings in Santiago are quite cold. So making arpilleras is not a matter of sewing a bit for pleasure and relaxation, or even for a little extra pin money; it is done out of sheer need and is therefore done in spite of very adverse conditions.

After some time I reached a point where I could talk intimately and frankly with women in two of the workshops, but I now find it impossible for me to describe adequately what the experience was like. I am unable to recreate the intense emotion of the real, lived experience. Some moments will have to remain sealed in my soul: the shared sorrow and pain when one or more of our companions was kidnapped; stories of torture and imprisonment, the double torment suffered by women — the usual treatment dealt out to all prisoners, and the extra pain, humiliation and degradation of sexual attacks. In the pages that follow I attempt to present a synthesis of what I heard and what I learned. I will re-tell some of the most striking, most unforgettable conversations I had with women who also belong to the Association of the Detained-Disappeared. The women of the Association workshop made the greatest impression on me because of the political direction their work has taken.

I came into the workshops as a visitor, a spectator, a listener. I brought along a tape recorder on a few occasions, but for the most part I just sat beside them to listen, chat, and watch them arrange their multicoloured scraps into colourful but searing pictures. At times they seemed to me like absorbed children, playing with a ragbag of treasures, concocting their tiny dolls, carefully dressing them in diminutive outfits, arranging their hair of yarn. I see them leaning intently over their work, exchanging colours. "Look, this will

70

go better on yours and you are so sad today, you should give the sky more colours."[1] They took me into their circle so I might listen to them; in return I told them about my life. Later I was accepted to such a degree that I could begin to ask them specific questions. I wanted to know what they thought about, what they felt as they sat sewing.

I had only to ask and a chorus of voices started to answer me all at once. They were eager to talk. "We are here to denounce what happened to us and to put our anguish into the arpilleras so others will know. Our first motive was to use our terrible pain to tell about our blasted lives."[2] Irma said that her first arpillera explained all her feelings. "I showed a shattered house, a destroyed building, a broken home, as my home has been since the disappearance of my son and daughter-in-law," she said. And it is true that her arpillera, made of torn scraps, bits of left-overs, tells a story that will survive loss and oblivion.

Another woman said, "I have made my arpilleras because I have a double crime to denounce, the kidnapping of both my son and my brother. For that reason I joined the workshop in order to continue fighting and so that the truth can be known because my wounds are still open." Over and over I heard the women refer to their drastic losses as though they were physical wounds, causing physical pain.

As we got to know each other better the women talked more and more openly of their great pain, the actual physical agony they felt and about their intense need to "live again," to regain a life that is genuine, real, truthful, to discover "the truth of their lives." The word *vida, life*, was forever in their speech: they constantly expressed their willingness to give "life for life," the hope "to find them alive" (*con vida*, in Spanish). Above all, their yearning, their hunger for simple, ordinary, normal life came out in the arpilleras — depictions of disappeared children playing when they were little, running carefree across fields and meadows as children everywhere do. At the same time, the women of these two workshops were strongly motivated to denounce those guilty of the crimes committed against their loved ones. Anyone who has seen their arpilleras will be touched by their powerful eloquence.

The search for loved ones goes hand in hand with the search for materials and colours to make the arpilleras. The long years of waiting and making of the arpilleras during this waiting has become a way of life for many of the women. The arpilleras are a constant dialogue with the missing; the relationship of the women with their creations has become both symbolic and symbiotic.

They say they get up in the morning and go immediately to the office of the Association, which has been given some space within the offices of the Vicarate. The arpillera workshops are scattered in churches throughout different neighbourhoods. Going to the office of the Association is a daily ritual, like their unceasing talk about their disappeared children, speaking of them as though they were present. I remember one winter evening Marisol and I were having a cup of coffee in a café in Santiago and she said to me, "I'm in a great rush these days knitting wool socks for Miguel, he can't go through the winter without wool socks." At that time Miguel had been missing for twelve years. (None of the women I met at the Association has ever found one of their relatives. And the search has gone on now for most of them for twelve years). Birthday celebrations are also regularly observed for the disappeared children. The whole neighbourhood is invited, making it a very festive occasion, just as if the missing one were present.

Inés says she has never been able to finish a single arpillera because her pain is too great. She doesn't know why, she says, but she just can't seem to finish one. The others try to encourage her, support her. They tell her, "Don't worry about it, here we are all family. We will manage it working together." And it is true that every workshop is a family, replacing in considerable measure the family that was lost when family members disappeared. Many friends and even relatives are afraid to associate with families of the dis- appeared, so sometimes those left behind lose everybody at once.

Hearing the women talk, especially those of the Association of the Detained-Disappeared, we noticed one theme kept recurring with particular insistence, and that is the story of the arrest of their

72

loved ones. The details are re-told, re-lived, repeated obsessively over and over. I never met one arpillerista who did not recount to me those moments. Each one told me how and where her child or relative was arrested, and about her continual, continuing search to find the missing one. Every search is the same. They all began at various known detention and torture centres such as Tres Alamos, Villa Grimaldi, Londres 38. As the women sit sewing they give details of their endless and fruitless treks. The responses they receive at the prisons are always similar: "You son is not here. We were told a few days ago he had left the country," or "Your husband has left you for another woman." To this date nothing is known of the fate of the estimated 10,000 persons who have disappeared in Chile since the coup in 1973 to the present, but for the arpilleristas the search is as much a daily routine for them as working on the arpilleras.

Irma tells me that she made a vow to herself that she would not let the jailers and prison officials see her break down, that she would not let them see her cry for anything in the world. "I am not going to cry when I ask for my son," she said. "You try to keep yourself strong while you're waiting your turn only to hear them say, 'Your son is not here.' Then I still won't cry and I leave with a big knot in my throat. To remember is very painful, I've gone ten years now with this open wound. Now, certainly, there are still disappearances, people disappear from off the street. The repression we are enduring has not ended. The first arpillera I made I remember as though it were yesterday. I remember I made a young woman, myself, pregnant with my son, then a long road filled with barbed wire and a black cloud. My arpilleras are very disturbing . . . I remember another one I made with much pain, one with my son as a little boy running across the sand on the beach, and in a little pocket on the back, I put a message that said, 'When I find my son, I will take him to the sea so he can run barefoot across the sand again.' In every one of my arpilleras I have spoken of pain but also of hope."

Victoria, sitting next to Irma, is sobbing but starts to try to tell me her story, which is also about the arrest of her son. She explains that her arpillera symbolized that event: "A tree crushed my son, a

73

tree full of flowers. I gathered one flower and rolled it down the road." I could fill this chapter with similar stories, because the stories of the arpilleristas are composed of similar memories, a collage, as María Eugenia called them, as she added her grief to that of the others: "I feel so much pain, they took away my only son. The very moment when the men came to my house asking for him he arrived from the University, came up the stairs, and they took him away. They said, 'Don't bother to come down, Señora. We'll bring him back to you before midnight.' Up to this day, nothing. (As of this year, 1986, her son has also been missing for twelve years. Author's note). Where have I not wandered, where have I not gone looking, banging on closed doors? I was almost out of my head. I wandered through the streets totally desperate. I even spoke with Lucía (wife of Pinochet) and she told me to come back the next day. But here we stay together. In Tres Alamos when they told me my son was there, I went out running so fast I bumped into a tree and broke my leg. (He was not there. Author's note). I became exhausted but we kept together here and I kept searching for him. My companions here have helped me. The arpilleras were a beautiful kind of therapy for me. The first one I made showed the disappearance of my son; it took me a month because every doll I made had something so despairing about it. I lived alone, coming back to my house to sew and to weep caused me great suffering. To relieve my anguish I made my arpilleras."

One day I asked the women to talk about how they got started making the arpilleras. Now we find it difficult to comprehend the proportions of this movement, to take in the impact it has had. Photographs of the arpilleras appear on calendars throughout Europe; the hangings have been exhibited in many countries, though not in Chile, of course, and this has all happened during the past thirteen years of repression and anguish.

They all tell me the same thing: they needed to earn extra money. "In the beginning the Pro-Paz Committee brought us little bits of yarn and scraps and we began to make dolls but they came out very stiff, but little by little everything was put together, the details appeared, and we began to see the world, so the arpilleras were born full of colours and full of stars."

It is enlightening to watch the women working together, interacting, to hear them tell of the events of their daily lives. Anita says, "Every morning I get up and go to the Association office to find out what's happening, what the others are doing." "Every one of us knows what is happening in her own sector," says María, from the East Zone. In this workshop I never saw any kind of hierarchical system. There are no monitors or directors who give instructions. The group chooses the themes to work on and makes all other decisions. They do offer help to each other, make suggestions about colours. They tell me, "Here in the workshop we tell jokes, we laugh, we cry and we console one another." Irma says, "There are no class differences here. We are a real family." Here I should explain that although 80 percent of the arpilleristas come from poor working-class families, with husbands either unemployed or missing, some 20 percent are from the upper-middle class who have joined the Association because of the disappearance of their children, or because they identify with the suffering of those who have lost family members.

As a kind of spin-off from the banding together of the membership in the Association, women seem to be cooperating in a new spirit. On October 30, 1985, 3000 women, representing a cross-section of all social classes, met in one of the affluent neighbourhoods of Santiago and marched silently together to the centre of the city to ask for a return to democracy. Before, only women from the shantytowns and poor neighbourhoods were participating in such marches, but now more and more women from all levels of society are joining them. Members of the Association participate as a matter of principle in virtually every such demonstration.

One day in the workshop I asked about what special feelings the women had when an arpillera was finished. They said, "a great anxiety at having to express openly all one's inner feelings, to have to sew and put together every detail, but happy to denounce what is happening." "When we finish our arpilleras our moods are clearly visible. When I am feeling sad, all my arpilleras come out in dark colours that show my loneliness."

Sometimes we talked about husbands, and it was obvious that their marriages were undergoing changes. They said, "In the beginning our husbands were against the workshops, they didn't want us to come, but now they take an interest and sometimes help us cut out the pieces for the dolls." One woman expressed what seems to be the transcendent fact of this movement of women occurring during a period of harsh oppression. She said, "The Chilean woman has to carry the whole burden, even peddling trinkets on the street up to the ninth month of pregnancy. Or think of the women at home alone with their husbands out of work, they have to figure out ways to bring up and educate their young children so they can believe in the dignity and worth of common people." Another woman said, "Women have changed so much that the military themselves made the comment that the biggest mistake they made was in leaving the family members of the *disappeared* alive."

In talking about how things had changed in her home, Amparo said, "The Chilean woman is playing the main role in the family today, and has also had to assume the role of provider for the family. Because of her double responsibilities changes have been made."

Through no fault of their own, men have lost their old position and status as breadwinner for the family, and traditionally men have never played a strong role in the day-to-day routine of the household. That was regarded as women's territory. Now the man feels exiled from both workplace and home. His frustration is evident as he tries various ways to escape, or at least alleviate, his painful situation. As might be expected, abuse of alcohol and suicide rates among men have risen substantially.

Once I sent a written inquiry to the women of various workshops asking them to describe the participation of husbands in workshops and related activities during the past decade. One answered, "They don't participate in anything, they are completely demoralized. They never go to the protests." Another explained, "It's much better not to send them to the protests. Why send them out so they can be sent into exile, or be arrested and killed?" Others expressed much tenderness in their replies: "When I am in a hurry to finish an arpillera everybody in the house helps me, even my husband when I catch him in a good mood." And another adds, "They help us make the heads of the dolls, it's very easy, or they stay with the kids when we come to the workshop."

This is not the first time in Chile's history that women have surged to the forefront of events. Some of these periods have been described in more detail in Chapter II. In recent times women started to play a wider role in public affairs during Allende's time. The intention was there on the part of the government, so to speak, but was never carried very far into practice. Now under the dictatorship a leading role has fallen to women almost by default, because of many different factors. A major factor is that the Junta, with its extreme attitude of *machismo*, takes men seriously but not women. Men have been their main prey for arrests, torture and disappearances. The Junta does not dare appear to take women seriously, no matter what they do. If a man joins a public protest against the regime, the Junta takes it as an open challenge to its authority that must be countered with whatever force is necessary. Women understand the precarious position of their husbands and also their own privileged position, so to speak, and have learned to take astute advantage of it. They not only denounce Pinochet's regime in their arpilleras, but in the streets as well. They have participated in all manner of demonstrations against the dictatorship. More often than not it is the women who insist that the men stay at home so they will not be arrested, exiled or tortured. Here again we see women assume the role of Super Mothers — protecting husbands and children, providing income to maintain the family, marching every Thursday to the building of the Supreme Court, wearing photos of their missing ones on their chests just as the Mothers of the Plaza de Mayo in Buenos Aires did — and still do. In Santiago the marches continue to take place in spite of police harassment and repression.

I ask them how they find the strength to do it all. They say, "We've been hit by so many blows in life. We might as well be out in the frontlines now because many of us have nothing more to lose." Another said, "Chile is a country divided by mountains but also

divided within. The arpilleras show, try to explain, this separation."
And another, "My life consists of making arpilleras but doing many
other things as well, such as going to visit political prisoners and
participating in any demonstration that might be going on and just
keeping faith with my people."

The women talked about their other activities as a group, their
demonstrations and political protests. They told me about various
protest actions they organized in 1979 outside of one of the largest
and most notorious torture centres, the one known as Londres 38,
from its address in downtown Santiago. (It is now a centre dedicated
to Bernardo O'Higgins (1776-1842), the liberator of the country).
The arpilleristas said they covered the walls of the house with a large
white cloth, sprinkled it with red paint to symbolize blood, and in
red paint wrote the names of the 119 prisoners known to have been
tortured there who later disappeared, meaning, of course, that they
were tortured to death and their bodies disposed of in some secret
place. As of today, no trace of any of their remains has been found. I
ask if they were afraid while taking part in that demonstration. They
said, "Afraid, no, in fact, just the opposite. That demonstration, like
the arpillera, is a way of saying what can't be said in any other
fashion, to tell what is really happening in our country. The fact that
we meet together here in the workshop is very important because we
give each other courage to go out in the street together."

They have all taken part in hunger strikes, have chained
themselves to fences in strategic locations in downtown Santiago
such as the Supreme Court, the door of Pinochet's house, the old
Casa de Gobierno. Many of their manifestations have disrupted
traffic and the normal flow of life in the Capitol — all are aimed at
calling attention to the Junta's practice of torturing and disappearing
people and are intended to force out the truth of what has happened
to the missing members of their familes. I ask again, What gives
them the strength to continue? What keeps them from faltering
against such odds? What drives them to undertake all this activity?
They said, "We still have hope to find our loved ones, if not alive, at
least to know the truth of what happened to them, and to recover
their bones if possible. but in spite of all, we feel they are still alive,

we feel their spirits everywhere." Delfina interrupts to say, "I believe my son is dead, but he lives on in the others, in all the young people. That is what keeps me alive and active. All the rest is secondary."

The Arpillera as Political Protest

I discuss here certain arpilleras that might be classified as chronicles detailing the crimes of the dictatorship. They can be "read" as easily as one reads a daily newspaper, so closely are they connected with daily events.

In my collection I have an arpillera that is unusual in that it bears a title on its reverse side: *Lonquén*.[3] It was made by Angélica after she went on a pilgrimage to Lonquén, a village on the outskirts of Santiago where a terrible discovery was made in 1978. A mass grave was uncovered inside an old abandoned mine shaft where remains of bodies of a number of farmers who had disappeared were found. They had been thrown into the mine shaft and then partially burned. After the discovery the Catholic Church organized a pilgrimage in which Angélica took part, along with many other members of the Association and thousands more shocked and saddened citizens of Santiago. Angélica's arpillera shows the macabre mass grave of Lonquén: in the midst of high mountains are several improvised ovens where human beings are burning. In this arpillera the event, the horror, the emotion, the hideous truth is all fused, but not in a way to provoke feelings of hopelessness and despair. It is rather intended to mourn the dead but also to celebrate the discovery of some part of the truth connected with the disappearances and to arouse families and their supporters to keep searching until all the truth is uncovered.

Hernán Vidal speaks of the transcendent nature of the pilgrimage to Lonquén. He writes: "The pilgrimage to Lonquén was a ritual of the celebration of life and therefore, an affirmation of the will and communal capacity to fight for a new society with clearness of purpose."[3]

María Cecelia tells me about another tragic event that was later depicted in an arpillera. In 1979 Sebastián Acevedo immolated himself in the main plaza of the city of Concepción (latitude 37° south). His two sons had disappeared and he had never received any response from the secret police as to their whereabouts or their fate. An arpillera shows Sebastián in his last moments surrounded by a crowd of people. Torn bits of newspaper are pasted to the design to show it was a real event. The immolation of Sebastián Acevedo gave rise to another movement: the Sebastián Acevedo Movement Against Torture. Some arpilleristas also belong to this group that carries out various public non-violent acts intended to recall his death and the reasons for it. Following are some of the chants that are repeated during the demonstrations. The initials referred to, D.I.N.A. and C.N.I., are acronyms for two notorious organizations of Intelligence and the Secret Police of Pinochet, that are most responsible for the kidnappings, torture and disappearances. *La Moneda* is the White House of Chile, where the head of Government lives and has his offices (where Allende was killed and where Pinochet now lives).

INVOCATIONS FOR SEBASTIÁN ACEVEDO

1.   Sebastián Acevedo, father, worker and prophet, on this anniversary of your immolation, we wish to remember you. There in Concepción, before the Cathedral, in the Plaza de Armas
TO STOP THE TORTURE, YOU ACCEPTED DEATH
Calling out "Let the C.N.I. return my sons to me . . ."
TO STOP THE TORTURE, YOU ACCEPTED DEATH.

2.   Sebastián, your immolation moved all of Chile and resounded throughout the world.
BUT THE REGIME KEPT ON TORTURING.
National opinion asked that the C.N.I. be dissolved.
BUT THE REGIME KEPT ON TORTURING.
The spokesmen for the regime were ashamed, averted their eyes and lied
BUT THE REGIME KEPT ON TORTURING.

3.   Sebastián, for an entire year your spirit has not been able to rest.

When we gathered in front of the clandestine prison of Borgoño
YOU WERE THERE
When we rattled the doors of the newspapers that remained silent
YOUR WERE THERE
When we pointed to those responsible: the torturers
of La Moneda
YOU WERE THERE
4. Sebastián, while Chile remains a territory of torture,
you will keep on grieving over our soil . . .
YOU WILL KEEP ON GRIEVING OVER OUR SOIL
But the day will come, Sebastián, it will come as sure as dawn,
when the night of death will sink into the abyss.
A NIGHT OF DEATH
and you will rest . . .
AND YOU WILL REST
And this Movement Against Torture that you helped create
will have completed its task . . .
WILL HAVE COMPLETED ITS TASK.

STRENGTH THROUGH SHARED LIVES

I discovered that the women of the workshops have emerged from their isolation of former years and together have learned to face the realities of life in Chile today. Their arpilleras ask for Bread, Work, and Liberty. The spirit of the women is very well illustrated by one of them who talked about the political protests. "At one time we all went with lighted candles through the centre of the city." Another added, "We told every bit of it on an arpillera, that has to be our way of denouncing. I have made the entire story of the disappearance of my son, and other mothers have done the same." "The arpillera cannot be prostituted for a thing that is not real." "We don't make the arpilleras just to be making something, to show little nothings or a field of flowers. The arpillera was born to show our real lives, disappeared children, hunger, unemployment, common soup kitchens, our lack of light and water."

I wish to recall some of the conversations I had with the arpilleristas of the East Zone workshop. Their experiences have not been as intense as those of the Association workshop since not all of them suffer the tragedy of the disappearance of family members, but they do suffer the very grave problems that have to do with simple survival—hunger and the fierce police repression inside the shantytowns. One said, "I'm not afraid to make arpilleras here in the workshop, but I am afraid to work on them at home because the cops come and trash everything." Another woman, speaking of the lack of light and water said, "When there is no light, I rustle up a few wires and steal a little, that's all." (Some arpilleras show the very common practice of "stealing" light by running wires from the house to the city light pole. The service has been cut off for non-payment of bills). In this workshop, composed of women 30-50 years of age, we have a cup of tea and a good laugh when Soledad says, "Who would believe that my arpillera was going to be in a boutique on Fifth Avenue (New York) when, imagine, I took a piece of blue from my own skirt to make the sky, from this ragged, cheesy skirt." We laugh again, but that description contains the real truth of the arpilleras; they are not a superfluous accessory; they are a form of art that comes out of daily life, the dailiness of life, down to the very clothes of the maker.

I ask the women how they feel now about the arpilleras after all these years. They say that at first they felt their work was very crude but now they feel more like artists or reporters describing scenes of daily life. One woman says, "I put an enormous sun in all my arpilleras, because even though I might not have a cup of tea to my name I never lose my faith."

Sometimes the women expressed their deep emotion about the arpilleras. One said, "My old man fell sick on me with his lungs, and on top of that he had cancer and landed in the hospital. I didn't know what to do so I decided to try to alleviate my anguish and made that the theme of an arpillera. I appliquéd a long road that went up to the hills and had no end, and there was a sun looking at me and the light gave me strength. The sun I embroidered entirely out of red yarn. When time came to sell it, I just couldn't. How was I going to sell that arpillera that had so much of myself in it? How could I think about setting a price for my own life?" Another woman added, "I have become so keenly fond of my arpilleras because they give me food but because they also help me kill my sorrows."

During my visits with the arpilleristas in the workshops and sometimes in their homes in the shantytowns, where a home is often a one-room shack for an entire family, with a cardboard roof, no light, water and naturally no bathroom, I most often found the women smiling, cheerful, with a contagious vitality. I asked them their ideas about God. I was not inquiring about a specific dogma or even about a specific religious belief. I just wanted to know what motivated them and kept them going. Many gave me basically the same answer. To quote one woman, "I see God as one who gave His life for a better world. He is present in each one of us. We have experienced the Way of the Cross because of our missing relatives, and the people who listen to our story, like you, for instance, in this moment, help us to bear this calvary." María's statement summed up the ordeal of the women in the workshops as well as the ordeal of Chile at the present time when she said, "God chose the humble to shame the powerful. It's for that reason we make the arpilleras so this kind of thing will never happen again."

THEMES OF THE ARPILLERAS

The arpillera is above all a form of popular art used to tell of personal experiences, but also to recount the tale of the tribe, in the way of ancient cultures. Like old sagas they tell of the trials and tribulations of the people, of heroes and villains, of courage and cowards, of struggle and survival. But instead of bards, balladeers or storytellers, an unlikely group has come forth to tell the story of Pinochet's Chile that was not supposed to be told. With left-overs and scraps, with found objects and rejects, torn pieces of newspapers, spent matches, the arpilleristas are methodically filling in what was intended to remain a blank in Chile's history. The arpilleras show the stuff of daily life for many people: hunger, sorrow, death, unemployment, repression, hope. The arpilleras are neither escapism nor political tract: they depict life in its complexity and contrasts. A smiling face and a sad one in the same arpillera—real life, in other words. Some arpilleristas have become quite sophisticated in their ability to express the sharp contrasts of life. One, for example, shows night and day — day hopeful with light and trees, night profoundly dark with all doors closed. The lack of water in poor neighbourhoods is a constant problem and is described over and over in the arpilleras. In one, children are shown playing near the school, the scene is lively and cheerful, but all the public water faucets have been Xed out with red yarn. In another a blue river runs through the centre of the arpillera but on the bank are children holding pails on which is written: "Give me water, we need water, please a little water."

Like all popular expression that departs from habitual forms and language, it is touching to see arpilleras with embroidered slogans and phrases with words misspelled. It is no wonder since some 60 percent of the women have received very little schooling.

Some arpilleras tell a connected narrative, simple stories such as one might find in a cartoon strip. A very successful one of this type has several scenes, one leading into the next, and the message is unmistakable. Strips of yarn close the door of the factory (unemployment) then we see children in a big common dining room (child feeding program) and women around a big outdoor common soup pot (food for the unemployed). The depiction of the church has become almost stylized over the years. Most often it is shown with little attached doors that open and close. Above the cupola there is always a big sun and next to the church door the common soup pot and a collection bag used to collect money on the streets to help keep all these projects going. The church always means food and hope.

During the first years of the dictatorship, 1973-1974, when the lives of so many had been shattered, designs of the arpilleras were also essentially unconnected fragments. Later after the women had become organized and had found some direction for their lives, the direction was reflected in turn in the arpilleras. The separate elements made up a whole, the world was being put back together again after a fashion.

One woman said that in one of her first arpilleras she showed her house. The door was open and inside the house she put flies, discarded papers, trash, because that's how her house was then. The arpilleras never stray far from reality. One Christmas scene shows Santa with a traditional white beard and a big sack on his back but the sack is filled with bread — there are no toys. The author of that one put down her real wish for Christmas. Another arpillera with a Christmas scene asks for "A Christmas With No Herods and No Torturers." Little by little the arpilleras have developed a language of their own, their way of saying things. One can discover a kind of semiotic shorthand of living experiences, some as simple as X's to show a building is closed or something not working. With time and practice some women have become very skilled and their work more thoughtful and sophisticated. I was impressed by one arpillera that shows a tree, a church and on the cupola of the church is written "Hunger Has Roots." This evolution of the arpillera to encompass a wider mode of expression has come about for two reasons: because the women have become more focussed as to their direction and intentions and their horizons have widened because of their activity. Their intent is to use the arpillera as an alternative way of communicating since normal channels are blocked. Such has been my observation about everything the arpilleristas who are also members of the Association of the Detained-Disappeared.

The first arpilleras dealing with the theme of the *disappeared* had a simple question mark embroidered over a figure representing the missing one. Then the question really was, Where are they? When will they be back home? Because at that time people believed they would return eventually. After more than a decade, that hope has faded if not died altogether, and the arpilleras have become sharper and more concrete. One carries the slogan: "TRUTH AND JUSTICE FOR THE DETAINED-DISAPPEARED" with a photograph of the disappeared one pasted to the cloth.

Photographs have become the talismans, the symbols of mothers looking for their missing children, whether in El Salvador, Argentina, Lebanon or Chile. The image keeps the memory real and alive, keeps the child close and is a comfort. The photographs says,

"Here it is, that's what he looks like, he exists."

As the women have accepted the task of telling by means of the arpilleras, their horizons have widened beyond their own personal sorrows to embrace those of other members of the group, the concerns of their neighbourhoods, and finally they are thinking of the agony of the country. The women who can read bring in newspapers and read stories of special interest to the others. One woman said, "Never in my life have I learned so much. I always regarded prostitutes as despicable and thieves as the scum of the earth, and now, well, I understand it's not their fault. I learned that here in the workshop."

From the practice of reading the newspapers came ideas for political protests, manifestions such as the ones recalling Sebastián Acevedo, or the idea of taking part in the pilgrimage to Lonquén.

Many arpilleras, especially those made in the last few years, express a longing for a better life in the future. Many show fields full of little animals and ripe crops surrounded by darkness. They tell me it is a dream of a better world, one with enough food for everybody. Another arpillera shows little girls celebrating their First Communion, the little dolls dressed in white lace like brides, a nostalgic scene, since the First Communion is a very happy day.

There are certain images that recur over and over. I would say that 90 percent of the arpilleras I have seen have a backdrop of the Andes. Sometimes they are very dark as though the mountains were in mourning. At times the peaks are gay and covered with flowers giving a hopeful air to the scene. The sun is another element that is very often present in the arpilleras, even in grim scenes such as those showing arrests. Perhaps one might argue that the Andes and the sun are a part of the realism of the arpilleras since the mountains are visible from virtually every location of Santiago and the weather is very often sunny and bright.

The arpilleras are a result of both intention and chance. The women begin with an idea of what they want to portray, but they must use whatever materials are at hand. Within these considerable limitations they achieve astounding expressiveness. Colour is one of their main ways to set the tone of a composition as is true in any visual art. The colour of the crocheted edging, the frame, and the large masses, such as the Andes, are chosen with as much care as possible to express the mood the women wish to convey. They tell me that grays and yellows lighten the scene and keep it from being too sombre.

Themes that occur very often in the arpilleras include the neighbourhoods, the houses, inside and out, signs of those missing, either disappeared or in exile, illustrations of the pick-up work they do to earn a little money — selling trinkets on the street (almost 90 percent of the women sell trinkets from time to time), working as street sweepers, washing clothes, working as maids. They often show the health centre, the common soup pot with a fire burning underneath, the child feeding centres, the closed school, lack of water and light, eviction scenes. Pilgrimages to remember the dead, protest demonstrations, torture centres, NO WORK AVAILABLE signs. The church and dreams. We have already mentioned the almost ubiquitous presence of the Andes and the sun.

Eduardo Galeano in his book, *Las venas abiertas de Latinoamérica* (The Open Veins of Latin America) writes, "In the system of silence and fear the power to create and to invent counters the routine of obedience."[4] This is without any doubt an important legacy of the arpilleras in Chile today, a legacy that is leading toward self-knowledge for the arpilleristas and a consciousness of worth for the working class in general.

The arpillera does not pretend to be a work of aesthetic coherence. The materials and methods used are, of necessity, extremely simple and modest. The stitches are uncomplicated, mostly chain stitch, blanket stitch and cross stitch. What is important is that real life is depicted with imagination and ingenuity, such as using a lock of one's own hair if necessary or a piece of one's own skirt to get a desired colour.

The arpilleras have a different quality from other needle crafts of Latin America that are intended for aesthetic pleasure only. Lucy Lippard is correct when she describes the arpilleristas in the following manner: "They protest the Junta's repressions and offer methods of self-determination and economic survival. These women can't sit around and analyse their role; it has been handed to them on a bloodstained platter. By confronting it in a familiar medium that does not separate art and life they are producing the most cohesive political art around. The arpilleras are the only valid indigenous Chilean art now that the murals have been painted over, the poets and singers murdered and imprisoned."[4]

Lippard is referring to the fact that during the Allende regime, schoolchildren, students, workers, in fact all citizens, were encouraged to participate in a project of drawing murals in the city parks and in other designated places. Many of these drawings were mildly didactic in that they illustrated the need for literacy or better health care, but on the whole, they simply were an attempt to foster a new social awareness. After the coup all the murals were washed off the walls or painted over and nothing is left of them now. It all happened so quickly almost no record is left of them. The most famous muralists were a group of students who called themselves the Ramona Parra Brigade and did extensive murals in the streets of Santiago, all vanished now.

Almost everyone is familiar with the fact that there were widespread arrests and exiling of artists and intellectuals after the coup. The folk singer Victor Jara was among the thousands rounded up in the soccer stadium immediately after the coup. He was murdered and when his body was claimed by his widow she found his hands had been mutilated. (He had accompanied himself on the guitar). Violeta Parra was already dead by the time the coup occurred but her children, Angel and Isabel, were exiled, along with literally thousands of others, among them the most gifted of the country's writers, artists and musicians.

In discussing (Chapter III) the possible antecedents of the arpilleras we mentioned a group of women called the Bordadoras de Isla Negra (The Embroiderers of Isla Negra). There is no doubt that the work of the women of Isla Negra, a farming and fishing village on the coast of Chile about 60 km. southwest of Santiago, had a great influence on the arpilleristas of Santiago. The success enjoyed by the Bordadoras, the great interest in their work abroad, the exhibitions in leading museums, including the Louvre, and sales of their work around the world provided a real stimulus for the arpilleristas. However, there are great differences in the work of the two groups and in the attitudes of the women toward their work. The most important difference is that the Bordadoras do not participate in any kind of public political activity. They seem to live outside current events in their protected rural retreat. Their attitude is undoubtedly due in large measure to the fact that they do indeed live in a tranquil area, in the country, sheltered from the horrendous problems and dangers that beset the shantytowns and poor neighbourhoods of Santiago on a daily basis. But there appears to be a will, a deliberate attempt to escape the convulsions occurring elsewhere in the country. During repeated visits to Isla Negra I noticed that when the names of very well-known Chileans arose in the conversation — Allende, Neruda, Pinochet — certainly the three most prominent public figures of Chile in recent years — the women never responded, they seemed not to have heard the comment. It's not that they are living in such an isolated area that they don't know who these men are. Neruda lived in Isla Negra off and on for thirty years, wrote about the embroideries and arranged the exhibit of them at the Louvre when he was Ambassador to France under Allende. Allende was known as a great admirer of their work and often presented the embroideries as gifts to foreign heads of state. We are left to conclude that their unwillingness to express any opinion that might be considered political is a form of self-protection. The women of the Santiago shantytowns, on the other hand, had no choice but to become politically active if they were to survive as whole, caring human beings. Their activism was thrust upon them by events.

In spite of differences, there are also similarities between the groups. Like the arpilleristas, the Bordadoras began their needle-work to earn extra income during the winter months when the Pacific is too stormy for the men to go to sea to fish and when there is no fresh produce for the market. As time went on the different groups of Bordadoras developed autonomous, independent ways of working; their work, especially the use of colour, became more and more expressive and imaginative. Now they have reached a point where their tapestries are internationally known and sought after. The women in CEMA CHILE workshops, described in the previous chapter, have been encouraged to produce counterfeit-bordados as well as counterfeit-arpilleras, and to try to pass them off as genuine autonomous folk art. But anyone who has studied the original works with even a little care can never be fooled by the fakes.

To give a little of the background of the Bordadoras, the work began in the 1960s, fostered by Doña Leonor Sobrino de Vera, a woman with philanthropic interests who lives part of each year in her home in Isla Negra. She wished to do something to ease the precarious economic situation of the villagers, particularly during the winter. As she herself describes the sequence of events, she was walking past a shop window in Santiago one day and saw a display of wool yarn of many varied and beautiful colours, and promptly suggested to some women in Isla Negra that they try their hand at making embroideries with wool yarn. Some were hesitant to try it, she says. Some had no skill at needlework. Nevertheless, with Doña Leonor's encouragement, they began to work anyway. At first they went out into the countryside and tried to capture the look of the landscape, the fields and trees. Later as they became more practiced and skilled, they progressed from landscapes to more varied scenes. They showed children playing games, men in their fishing boats, animals and birds, the sea, and also imaginary scenes. One might say they show life as it ought to be, as the women dream it, or remember it, not as it actually is.

The technique employed in making the embroideries is much finer and more elaborate, more time-consuming that that used for the arpilleras. The stitches are varied, the mix and shading of the colours sometimes inspired. Embroidery covers the entire surface of the backing cloth so that the finished work has the look of a woven tapestry, or a painting. The arpilleras are like a newspaper sketch; the embroideries like naive paintings, with their brilliant colours and childlike disregard for the regular rules of perspective and proportion. There are birds bigger than the houses over which they are flying, a threshing scene within a circle as though seen from above, and the other elements of the scene also seem to be airborn, revolving around the central picture. However, the intent of the embroideries is to be true to the inner vision of the maker, and the many small details help create a true expression of a luxuriant landscape, the sea, and the life of the village.

The women of Isla Negra work mostly in the winter, sitting beside the fire, dreaming of spring and summer, remembering scenes from childhood, and thus they reproduce the houses and scenes of years ago. So a true portrait of Isla Negra comes through, but Isla Negra remembered.

The arpilleristas, on the other hand, show what happened to them yesterday, or last night, or what they saw this morning. Police sweeps. Arrests. Beatings. Hasty burials of dead prisoners at night in unmarked graves. Or they show what they see every day: soup kitchens, closed factories, women washing clothes, children playing. And there are the constants in their life: the church, the Andes, the sun, the *disappeared*.

I asked the women in Isla Negra if they had heard of the arpilleristas in Santiago or of other groups who have become known for needlework like embroiderers of Macul and Conchalí. These embroideries are also of wool and use the same technique that the women from Isla Negra use, but the work has not become as well known yet. They said yes, they had heard of these groups, but offered no further comment. They show no inclination to venture out of their protected and beautiful corner of the world, and who can honestly blame them? May they continue to live and work as always and to delight us with their idyllic and aesthetic view of a world that should be.

The lives of the Bordadoras is contained by their families, nature, the seasons of fishing and farming. I ask them how they pick the scenes to embroider and one woman replies, "I made my house with all the trees and flowers and plants. At first we didn't have much self-confidence but Doña Leonor helped us."[6] Another said, "I felt really afraid making my first embroidery, but Doña Leonor liked it a lot."[7] I never encountered this feeling of being afraid and anxious about how the work will come out and be received among the arpilleristas of Santiago. Perhaps this is a major difference between a popular art made for aesthetic purposes only, that is, art meant to please, and art meant to expose and denounce, like the arpilleras.

Both groups reflect in their work the world they live in: the tranquil world of farms and sea of Isla Negra where harshness comes more from nature than from man, and the world of the arpilleristas of Santiago, under constant siege where life is precarious in all respects, a nightmare world. We can only admire the fearlessness and courage of the arpilleristas who choose to confront the evils and demons of their world, to denounce them and fight them not only in their pictures but in the streets as well.

There is one important aspect that both groups have in common — the joy and comfort they find in working together with other women. The Bordadoras spoke warmly of how much at peace they are in their familiar surroundings and the pleasure they get from the loving friendships that have developed among women of the groups. Both groups work cooperatively and on equal terms with one another, without leaders or monitors. In both cases the more experienced women help the newer members of the group. Both the arpilleras and the embroideries have become known and prized far beyond the borders of Chile — a tremendous achievement for any artisan, a transcendent victory for the housewives and mothers of Isla Negra and Santiago. By working seriously with modest means they have made an impact on Chilean society and changed their lives in the process.

FOOTNOTES

1   All direct quotes come from members of the Association of Families of the Detained-Disappeared.

2   For the protection of the women they have been quoted as a group, "they", or invented first names have been used.

3   There is an interesting book of Máximo Pacheco called *Lonquén* (Santiago: Aconcagua, 1980) which gives the history of this event. A fictionalized version appears in Isabel Allende, *De Amor y de Sombra* (Of Love and Shadow) Barcelona: Plaza & Janes, 1984. Also see Hernán Vidal.

4   Eduardo Galeano, *Las venas abiertas de latinoamérica (The Open Veins of Latin America)*, México: Siglo XXI, 1977 edition, p. 20.

5   Lucy R. Lippard, *Get the Message: A Decade of Art for Social Change.* New York: E.P. Dutton, 1984, p. 86.

6   Statement of Narciso Catalán, Isla Negra, July, 1983.

7   Statement of Alicia Pérez, Isla Negra, July, 1983.

CHAPTER 5

TESTIMONIES

The testimonies that make up this chapter are presented exactly as they were received by the author. No attempt has been made to correct small errors or to reconcile variations that may exist in different versions of the same event. The translator, working in close collaboration with the author, has made a special effort to capture the emotional feeling of the original accounts. Punctuation has been kept the same since the original writing clearly indicates the flow of a story that is being told, and has been told over and over, rather than a narrative composed especially for publication. Occasionally an explanatory word or phrase has been added for the sake of clarity. Although names and biographical details are mentioned in many of the testimonies, we have left the accounts unsigned in an attempt to protect as far as we are able the brave women who have dared to tell us their stories.

Testimony #1

... I was born in Chile, a country of mountains, three hundred years of struggle did not save us from the conquest and independence from Spain did not save us from madness.

My interest in art arose naturally from my contact with other students, in the face of family opposition I entered the school of Fine Arts in the University and there became involved in movements interested in working with community groups, in literacy work in marginal sectors of the city, finding for the first time the gratifying sensation of giving something and not only that but contributing something of great value to others, such as the ability to read and write.

This short period of work in the poor neighbourhoods was a great help for me in defining many things in my life, the coming in direct contact with different social classes and opportunities, such different rights, such a different sense of justice from one side to the other, and yet so equal in the right to life and to love.

Slowly I entered a period of personal confrontation with myself, of questioning. Trying to be aware above all of the fact of being a woman, I began to work with women.

Together we began the search for our own cultural roots, those that were most pure, the least contaminated ones, the women learned to value and to feel pride in their past and in their origins by showing their work, in that way recuperating their lost self-esteem. We were happy they and I.

But we are not only our origins, we are our origins plus everything that happens in our history, we are the result of three hundred years of struggle, we are the result of the cultural influence and the slow impoverishment of our land, of the importation of luxurious goods that we don't need, of the propaganda that transforms us into a society that consumes products that we don't make, of seeing every day on television a luxurious and exotic life that we try to imitate and in that way we again repeat the cycles of our earlier history when we embraced foreign cultures and values instead of treasuring our own.

As an artist I am the mixed result of my history, my actions, my process and my commitment. Based on my commitment I have carried out a long and varied career trying to open other areas that are less individualistic, to find other possibilities of expression. Especially since as artists we have always provided the testimony of our epoch.

And here I wish to speak about a part of my work, the arpilleras. Their beginning, their expression, their possibilities and their future.

After the military coup I was out of a job like so many others, in a short time the Pro-Paz committee asked me to develop some craft work projects with women, the first group assigned to me were women of families of the detained-disappeared: mothers, wives, sisters. At the end of my first interview with them, it was clear to me that in their state of anxiety they would not be able to concentrate on anything except their own pain, I went back to my house, their anxiety embedded in me, I could hardly believe what I had heard, sons, husbands, brothers snatched with blows and threats to their families, pregnant women carried off, couples including their small children, all disappeared for weeks and even months, with nobody knowing anything about them, not even about the newborns cr the older children and even less about the adults.

Everything I had been thinking of doing with these women was useless, since the future work we would undertake together ought to serve as a catharsis, every woman began to translate her story into images and the images into embroidery, but the embroidery was very slow and their nerves weren't up to that, without knowing how to continue I walked, looked and thought and finally my attention was attracted by a Panamanian *mola*, a type of indigenous tapestry, I remembered also a foreign fashion very much in vogue at that time: "patchwork." Very happy with my solution the very next day we began collecting pieces of fabric, new and used, thread and yarn, and with all the material together we very quickly assembled our themes and the tapestries, the histories remained like a true testimony in one or various pieces of fabric, it was dramatic to see how the women wept as they sewed their stories, but it was also very enriching to see how in some way the work also afforded happiness, provided relief, happiness to see that they were capable of creating their own testimony, relief simply from the fact of being together with others, talking together, sewing, being able to show that by means of this visual record others would know their story.

This *collage* of fabric, mixture of *mola* and patchwork, was not, as a technique, new, but we all liked it and were satisfied with it. Some visitors and foreign journalists saw the result and took them away, other people, all motivated by our problems, acquired them and they began to be in demand inside the country as well as abroad, the demand for the arpilleras had begun.

Two months after beginning this work, seeing the results, Pro-Paz assigned me to other groups, the economic model imported from Chicago by the military regime began to cause havoc, this time among industrial workers. Unemployment was going up, imported goods arrived by the tons, propaganda helped turn us into a grossly overblown importer-country. And with this primitive streak that still remains in us to be dazzled by glass beads of beautiful colours, we bought and bought without realizing that by doing so we were closing down our own industry, and as our factories closed there were hundreds and thousands of unemployed workers and the workers had wives and children and all of them needed to eat.

The Church assumed a historic role, opening its doors and taking on as its own the problems of the most needy. In a desperate attempt to stave off malnutrition the first childfeeding problems were begun in various churches. The mothers in the communities organized, going out every morning to collect left-over foodstuffs, from stores, private houses, restaurants, in produce markets, even going out into the countryside and there gathering produce of poor quality that could not be sold in the markets, it was painful to see how few resources they had to work with, many times, the good half of a half-rotten tomato was used, and the same thing went for potatoes and other vegetables and fruits, it was an impressive effort to cook something with the poor and miserable things they were able to collect.

Then we saw heartbreaking situations when women recently confronted by the drama of hunger would arrive at the church dining rooms for the first time with their children, only to find all the places taken, but it never failed that some woman would give up her place to the newcomer saying "My child ate yesterday and the day before, let your child eat now."

That was the atmosphere I found when I arrived, and these things I am telling I learned from the women there, I began to take real account of the unemployment and the effect produced by the continuing closing and more closing of factories.

Also there were anguished women, another kind of anguish, first of all, hunger, and another equally painful, to see a child slowly becoming thinner and thinner, slowly being consumed, not having means to go to a hospital, nothing with which to buy medicine, is always painful. And with these groups the story of the arpilleras continued.

The women didn't know how to begin, one of my volunteer companions, Gloria Torres, a lawyer, suggested to the children that they draw the dining rooms, new collages of fabrics appeared with enormous pots, enormous tables filled with children and long lines awaiting their turn, these were the things they began to tell in different arpilleras, then they began to make their own drawings, mamas collecting foodstuffs, cooking, serving steaming hot plates, mamas waiting. We should add here that the only income some of these women received at all was from the sale of arpilleras.

This experience was very successful and I was sent to another quarter, also a marginal working-class neighbourhood, where there were other women with different problems but with one in common: unemployment. Meeting not in a church but in a chapel, the chapels of our poor neighbourhoods are also poor. Small constructions of 3 x 6 metres, up to 6 x 12 metres for the largest.

Our little chapel served us as child-care centre, dining room, as a place for mass, for the catechism, for baptisms, as a meeting place, as a place to ease one's sorrows.

One of the groups of women had formed a little laundry service when their husbands lost their jobs, washing clothes is work that women in our shantytowns know how to do well, with no washing machines washing is done by hand in a tub, it is also very common that the houses have no running water and water has to be carried in buckets from some nearby faucet, the children are expert water carriers and the women too have very strong backs for carrying loads. The laundry business didn't go very well because by now the men of the middle class were starting to lose their jobs and their wives had to take on the domestic chores, so that with the increase in unemployment the numbers of women wanting work washing clothes went up while the clientele went down. In view of this situation I was called in to see what I could do with this group, and other arpilleras appeared telling other stories. These women were very imaginative and began the evolution of the arpilleras, incorporating volume and other materials to the work, it was very heart-warming to see reflected in the new arpilleras the very busy little chapel, and so much laundry hanging on the line. In addition to picturing the stories of the women washing clothes they told how their husbands had lost their jobs when the factories and plants had closed, of the interminable treks that the men made in search of work, of how they slowly used up their few possessions, of the solidarity that developed around the common soup pots. Other artists began to be inspired by this experience and that's how the theatrical work called "Tres Marías y una Rosa" (Three Marías and a Rose) came about.

Many other groups were formed from the arpillera groups, carrying out different activities, within the limits of my possibilities.

Finally four years ago and at my request I entered the Missio foundation, this time I had a different perspective, the experiences we had had together were thought of as of a transitory character, but six years after the coup unemployment was still high and growing more acute, and for that reason the new workshops that were formed had to be transformed into permanent organizations, meaning they were confronted with new technical problems, with commercial and production questions that would demand new judgements regarding expenses and administration, to which neither the workshops nor the support staff were prepared to respond.

The executive secretary of the Missio foundation, Sister Karoline Mayer, gave me a vote of confidence. I started working in a sector of the North zone where unemployment reached 70 percent and fear 80 percent. The workshops were filled with women who were neurotic, allergic, depressed, who lived only in the present. Slowly we assembled craft and organizational people to staff the 20 workshops that were formed there, three were organized to make arpilleras, each one according to their own inclination. The more serious ones spoke of the problems of their neighbourhoods: the ripped-out water and electric meters, the ramshackle condition of the latrines with the corresponding invasion of flies, the accumulations of trash and drug addiction.

The most Christian ones speak of how one keeps to one's faith in the shantytowns, of the persecution today that is similar to that imposed by the Pharoahs on the Israelites, how the persecution of Christians continues, of how Christ's word is transformed into subversive discourse, they speak of that faith that obliges one to help the neediest, of the faith that lives asking for understanding, of that faith that is sustained by the love of one for another. The most timid ones speak of the city, the city of important buildings and the surroundings, of the colonial era church, of its beggars and passersby, of the other big Church where one of the walls holds a municipal permit for a Persian fair, of our church with its bus stop, its miraculous Virgin and newspaper kiosk, of the markets, of the railroad stations, they also speak of the history of the workshops and their organization, of that organization that has changed their lives, that has converted them all into individuals, of that organization that changed them into a self-run enterprise, that manages three commercial outlets, that lets them face life in a different way, freer, more independent, with fewer economic problems; and the most important is that the organization made them discover the value and strength of a community.

Testimony #2

I worked as a seamstress, was an apprentice in a tailor shop when my son started to school. Since I was alone, in order to educate him, I went to work in a private house as a maid. There were other children in the house. When he was five, I took him to school and picked him up and worked late to be able to make up the time.

The boy had very good grades so he went to the National Institute which is very good. I had to do a lot of chores. Later he applied to the University of Chile, to the Engineering School, he was very intelligent. He received one of the highest scores. I was very proud of him.

He was always a very good student and when he entered the third year of his professional studies, he was named assistant professor. So that in addition to studying he was working. When he got his first paycheque he embraced me and said, "Mamita, now you don't work any more, now I will support you." Fifteen years I worked to educate him.

We rented a little house, a modest one, my son gave me all his salary to pay the rent and the expenses. I convinced him to let me work half-time, I wasn't accustomed to working so little. So we went along buying what we needed and set up our home.

When he was in his fifth year of study he won a fellowship to study in Sweden, I cried from sadness, never had I been separated from him since he was born, but he said to me: "Mamita, if it's for my benefit, and the time will go flying by." It wasn't true but I consoled myself reading the cards and letters he sent me every day from Sweden.

He returned and went on with his studies and received his degree. That day we were both so nervous and it gave me so much pleasure when he handed me his diploma. "Now I'm an engineer," he told me.

He applied for a job with the National Railways organization. He was hired immediately and years later when President Allende came to power he was one of three to be considered for the position of director of the company. When he was selected we threw a party in our house to celebrate. We were both of us so happy and proud. "I'll give you everything Mamita," he said, and kept his promise. We moved to a pretty chalet in a good neighbourhood and in a little while there were all kinds of conveniences. I felt that my mission as a mother was completed.

But then the coup came and everything was shattered, since my son was a top executive he was fired a week after the coup. As for him it didn't affect him all that much. He immediately started to work with another engineer on their own and went about freely everywhere.

But I was very distressed, I begged him to go into exile, but he told me he had to fight here. He helped his friends who were in bad shape and carried them clothes, sheets, blankets, I went with him to the poor neighbourhoods.

And on the 4th of March of 1975 they took him away from me. They were waiting for him in the house, when he arrived in his car they took him away. I thought that those men who were waiting for him were friends of my son, he didn't come back after night came, and never had he stayed out overnight, I almost died.

The next day I went to the Pro-Paz committee, there were other women there in the same situation. I spoke with the social worker, with the lawyer, and cried. I told them that without my son I wasn't going to be able to go on, that I would die. I asked myself why? Why? I was crazy, sick, undone, I cried all day long in the streets.

I wanted to kill myself if my son didn't come back within six months. But later my companions there told me to resign myself, that we all had the same pain, that they were suffering the same.

So my fight began, I said to myself I had to survive this blow because I have to know where my son is and I have to see that man fall who is in the government.

The other women of the Association of the Detained-Disappeared welcomed me very warmly and I began to gain strength and courage and began to take all the legal steps possible after the detention of my son.

A lawyer made the appeal for the protection of civil rights (Recurso de Amparo) that I personally carried to the Supreme Court. I began to make the rounds of all the hospitals, the morgue, the SENAE, the Psychiatric Hospital, the International Red Cross, the different detention centres, I covered all the jails of the zone.

At this time the Association of the Detained-Disappeared had a van for the use of us family members who were searching for a detained one. Through the Vicarate of Solidarity we could talk with other political prisoners and ask them if they had seen my son, we took photos for them to see when we made our inquiries.

That's how I knew my son was detained in Villa Grimaldi. Six people swore before a minister of the court that they had seen him there, that he was all right, that he hadn't been tortured, but one night they had him say good-bye to his friends because he was being released, and since then nothing more has been known of him up to this date.

I ask myself, where have they got him? In a secret prison? I think they may have him working somewhere because he is so intelligen.

With the women of the Association we got organized and began to make different actions to denounce our situation and to obtain a response about our family members.

I took part in a hunger strike, with the objective of pressuring the government and finding out where our loved ones are. This strike took place in the month of June, 1978. For 17 days I lived only on water and salt. The first week I felt well but beginning on the eighth day I began to weaken and worsen to such a point they were forced to feed me intravenously in order for me to survive and they administered extreme unction.

Those in the government promised to tell the truth if the hunger strike was ended, because they were told that several women were gravely ill and that if any of them died they would be responsible but to this day they have said nothing.

I also participated in a protest action in which we chained ourselves to the fence at the Supreme Court Building and as a result we were detained five days in the House of Correction. They took all of us who had participated.

I reflected on my moments of happiness when I was with my son and my moments of loneliness when they took him away from me, and these I put in images in the arpilleras.

I reflected about my life, how much I had sacrificed to educate my son. Just when I was going to be happy, just when I no longer had to work, this happened and all the anguish came to me that I showed in the arpilleras.

I felt happy to show the arpilleras to other people because they find them moving and beautiful and the work says what we want it to say.

Later we talk about our daily activities in the Association of Families of the Detained-Disappeared, the actions we took when we went to the Tribunals, to jails where we spent days at a time in case I might see my son.

We also denounced other problems, not just our own problems, but unemployment, the massacre of Lonquén, the shantytowns, how people live there, the soup kitchens, the closed factories, children begging, so that people living outside in the world will see how we live here. We are also concerned about the problems of other people, with all that we see and feel and that we show in the arpilleras. With other arpilleristas we discuss our themes, we show our work to one another. There were some women there before I arrived and they were very strong and helped me to survive the crisis of the first moment. Now I still suffer but I know how to control myself, I have companions with whom I can talk and feel that we have the same pain.

In the Association of Families of the Detained-Disappeared we have frequent gatherings and day-long discussions in which we analyze specific problems of the group, the lack of constancy of some people in attending, of doing things so that people will start attending again. I have never stopped attending the meetings, the Association has become my family, we have an office and going there is like going to your own house.

I now live from the pension I have which is something like 5,000 pesos ($50) a month and from the work of the arpilleras which is another thousand and a bit. But I'm a real "hustler" and am always looking for things to do, because when they arrested my son I was left with nothing, I even had to sell the television.

Ever since my son was born I had him by my side until they took him away from me. Now he would be some 40 years old. I have the hope that my son will return and that I will see him, I think they have him somewhere and that he's alive, I never want the thought to pass through my head that they have killed him.

I think, Why couldn't they have condemned him to 15 or 20 years of prison so that I could visit him?

Many times I have felt when I was sleeping that he was saying Mommy Mommy. I say to him my dearest son, may God bless you, protect you, be with you.

BIOGRAPHY

ALFREDO ROJAS CASTAÑADA, I.D. card No. 4.019.953-5 of Santiago, Enrollée No. 4941 of the College of Engineers of Chile. Married, 3 children. Born the 22nd of September, 1940 in Santiago. Began his first studies in Public School No. 23, then entered the National Institute where he finished his secondary studies. An outstanding student he completed his studies in 1958, and later entered the School of Engineering of the University of Chile, receiving a degree in electronic engineering in 1965. Later entered the National Railways, where he worked in the Department of Electrification.

In the year 1967 he won a merit fellowship to study at the ASEA company in Sweden, and spent six months there.

He worked in the National Railways Agency until 1968, left to work on his own until 1971, in which year he was asked by the Government to fill the position of Director General of the Department of National Railways, a post he occupied until September, 1973.

After that time he returned to working on his own and at the same time continued his work as an activist in the Socialist Party of Chile, in the Cordillera Regional Section; the 27th of September, 1974 he was arrested for the first time, remaining 10 days in the torture centre of the Headquarters of the National Intelligence Organization located in José Domingo Cañas Street, after those 10 days he was released. He continued with his work as an engineer and as an activist of the left until March, 1975, when he was DETAINED for the second time by men from D.I.N.A. when he returned to his house in his own car, a Yagan Citroen, beige colour, black top, motor NA 50300-5187 Chassis No. 00145, that had been seen by members of his family occupied by unknown persons.

ALFREDO ROJAS CASTANADA was active in the Socialist party, of which he was one of the directors, from the time he was 18 years old, because all his life he worked for the cause of the People, of the oppressed, he was son, father, exemplary husband.

This event and many other examples will never be explained in real and concrete detail, without the solidarity and pressure of people who are brothers to the Chilean people, we demand that the military Junta of Chile tell us the truth.

Testimony #4

Santiago de Chile 28 February, 1985

I received your letter dated the 14th of this month, and a few days later a card, I haven't answered you because I wasn't in Santiago, I went with my husband on a little vacation to the South, so that when I got back I had your letter, so I went to work immediately, it was a bit hard for me to get inspired because I came back too relaxed from the trip, to be with people there is as though they lived in another world, things don't happen to them such as we in the Capitol see and live every day.

At the same time I send this letter, I will send the order so hoping you will like it, as I told you earlier in every one of my works I put my life because I make my arpilleras thinking about all the immense painful problem here, in every pore of my being, and it hurts me every day the same way, it's not true that one forgets with time, perhaps when things happen in a natural way, but not the way it happened with my son Jorge. I could talk so much about this but I won't any more because I don't want to infect you with my sadness.

That's very good what you tell me about the article on the Association, I do hope you can send it, they would thank you many times over because we receive that type of material very rarely.

As for the orders in the future I believe it would be possible in general to send them from the workshop but we stumble against the problem that there are people in great need and they want to have their money immediately, it would be good if we could find a way to do it.

Thank you for considering me your friend, I hope you realize it is the same from my side.

With a big and affectionate embrace.

Testimony #5

Santiago de Chile 8 April, 1985

I am a bit ashamed that I haven't written you earlier but you know all our daily activities, and at times I don't understand how the day flies by and I don't get around to doing all I planned to do, that happens to me with letters, every day I think I'll sit down and write, but as you see I never get beyond the thought, I hope you understand and don't think that it's only a "little white lie," all the events of the country make us aware of one thing after another, at this moment the treacherous assassination of those people. (The writer is referring to the murder of three people, two of them teachers, in 1984. Their bodies were found dumped beside the road, their throats cut.) How could anybody as a human being stay here just as if nothing had happened, we are looking for ways to denounce the horrible nightmare that we have been suffering during all these years. At times I feel there is such great indifference that I am filled with desperation, how to shake up the people and say to them WAKE UP SHITHEADS, pain makes you think so many things and say so many things and do so many things, things that one wouldn't do ordinarily.

Changing the subject I'm happy you received my package since I was worried that perhaps it didn't get through, but finally now it is in your hands, the contents consist of ME my life, my thoughts, my dream revolves around the question WHERE ARE THEY? a question I will keep on persuing until the jackals answer; is the face of the sleeping person so beautiful that you thought it was a child? Truthfully I would prefer that my work not need an explanation, that just by looking at it one could see what it means. Regarding your question about whether we could do a special arpillera all together in the workshop, I have to explain to you that we can hardly work at all these days because with the Earthquake the office where we work in the North Zone was left in a totally delapidated state, most of us in the Association suffered serious damage in our houses, in my house the greater part of the roof fell to the ground and cracks appeared in various parts of the house, but I think that mine is nothing compared to what the people suffered who lost everything.

Concerning what you say about the testimony of my daughter I will try to do it, it is very painful, so many things have happened during my search for her, the pain is so great, the humiliations, the ridicule, at this moment just to say I will do it makes me feel a terrible knot in my throat and I can't stop crying, but I will do it even if it hurts me.

My dear friend this brings a big embrace full of love.

Testimony #6

TESTIMONY
By the Mother of the DETAINED-DISAPPEARED,
JORGE MULLER SILVA
Detained the 29th day of November, 1974
together with his fiancée
CARMEN CECELIA BUENO CIENFUENTE

After living so many years in a dictatorship and having suffered during nearly all those years the disappearance of a loved one, one almost forgets how to write, there are so many thoughts of pain, of anguish, of rage and impotence that it is as if the senses only whirled round and round all those events, I live my life thinking, What to do? How come out of this black pit called Chile, it seems that everything I do amounts to nothing, it is as if one were trying to hold a drop of water between the fingers. I don't know where to begin to say all that has happened to me since they arrested my son and made him disappear, I don't believe there is enough paper in the world to tell what those years have been like.

My son Jorge was a movie cameraman and completed his studies in the Film School of the University of Chile in Viña del Mar, even before he completed his studies he began to work in la Cámera (a film-making group) making documentaries on political events during the time of the Unidad Popular (United Popular Front). In 1970 he made a tour to various European countries

107

covering the visit of the then Minister Sr. Clodomiro Almeyda (under Allende) he had a permanent job, even after the military coup, at the beginning of 1974 he filmed his last movie in the north of Chile "A la sombra del sol" (In the Sun's Shadow). On the 28th day of November, 1974 the movie was shown in Las Condes Theatre in the elegant quarter and there were even members of the military in the audience. Seeing the picture I felt so proud of what my son had done I said to my husband, "Jorge has a great future ahead of him," how could anyone think that that night would be the last time we saw him, when the movie was over we came out into the foyer and he told us, "I won't come home tonight, because we are going to celebrate the success of the picture." We didn't ask him where he was going, but later when I began to search for him we know he was with a girlfriend, the whole group was there, they stayed there all night and the next morning two men came to my house to ask for him when I asked them who they were they said they were companions from work, later I realized they weren't companions, then when quite a bit of time had passed and I began to know what they were like in general the guys who made the arrests, especially one who arrested so many young people during those years and whose name is ROMO, at this moment I can't recall the rest of his name, it's as though I wanted to erase it from my memory, and on the other hand I know how important it is not to forget it.

The 29th of November, 1974 since my son Jorge and Carmen were supposed to go to Chile Film and never arrived I began to make telephone calls asking for him, I wasn't too worried because I talked to one of his friends who told me that it seemed they had all gone to the beach, but nevertheless I had my doubts, I personally didn't know the problem of the Detained but Jorge always told me what was happening. To tell you the truth I almost didn't want to believe everything he told me, I thought I had always admired the armed forces, but more than that since I have two half-brothers who have retired from the Carabineros (the Chilean Police force concerned with civilian affairs) with the rank of Captain, I felt in that case if Jorge had been arrested only because he had a different opinion surely they would try him, that's what the Courts are for. In addition because of our economic situation, and because I have a brother-in-law who works for the United Nations in Chile in a high position, the thing (with Jorge) wouldn't go any further, how many families there were like me, thinking and believing the same, because never had anything similar happened in Chile. When there was finally no doubt whatsoever about his arrest a friend told me to go to the PRO-PAZ COMMITTEE that had been in operation since the coup giving legal assistance to those detained, from that time this calvary began, every visiting day at the concentration camp of Tres Alamos I was there, asking if he was detained, sometimes the guards told me yes he is here and has a visitor, and when it was my turn to enter they would say no he's not here he hasn't been arrested, naturally the camp full of armed carabineros, one had only to come a little closer than what was allowed and they would put a gun barrel between your eyes as though ready to fire, in the concentration camp I was able to talk one time with a Lieutenant whose last name was Zabaleta, he was a military lieutenant I didn't know his given name, this man making me believe that he was friendly said to me I'll go inside to ask if your son is in detention, later he came back naturally with the reply that he was not there, I continued to go to Tres Alamos until July or August of 1975 more or less half a year with the hope that they would tell me where they had taken him, I went to SENDE (acronym for a military centre of information) that was an office where supposedly they gave information about those detained, every day I went to ask for my son, in this office there were the four branches of the armed forces, you had to sign, leave your identity card, later they went through the act of going to look at some lists that their superiors had and naturally came back every time with the same reply, also in this office there was a social worker who according to them was supposed to aid the women who were prisoners and were released, her name is Raquel Lois, also there was in this office Jorge Espinosa Ulloa a member of the military, on one occasion he received me he also told me my son had not been detained, that most likely he had left the country as so many had done, among other things he told me, he said "that the action justifies the means." How could I forget it? and when I left he held out his hand, I didn't know whether to take it or spit on it. On another occasion I went to the Ministry of Defense, I already knew that the Head of D.I.N.A. was general Manuel Contreras Sepúlveda, I went there and asked for an interview with Manuel Contreras, but the Contreras who came was a much higher general who had nothing to do with D.I.N.A., then he said "I'm not the one you are looking for but go to the floor below and ask to speak to the general So-and-So." At this moment I have forgotten the name but I have it written down somewhere because I remember very well what this general told me, after I waited for him a long time in a large foyer where men in uniform were coming in and out I watched with a lot of attention then they took me to a small room so I couldn't see any more, then came this general, I explained to him what I was looking for, then he told me that it wasn't D.I.N.A. but the Secret Service of the military for the military, he asked me how old my son was I told him 26 years old, then he told me why are you worried if your son is just a Mama's Boy — imagine — and then I became furious and asked him if he had children, and if he was going to consider them Mama's Boys when they were grown, I said where was the love of a father to consider that the children didn't always need a mother, I spoke to him of the pain of the Virgin Mary in seeing her son crucified, I know I disarmed him morally in that moment, but I found out nothing. I sent letters to all the members of the Junta to whatever general was assuming some post in the government from all or nearly all I received a reply but always the same, that my son had not been detained by orders from that Ministry, I sent a letter to Lucía (Pinochet) appealing to her love as a mother and the reply she sent me was that "you should turn over the information to the pertinent agencies" up till today, after the rage kept building and building up in me and the pain so strong that by then I didn't want to write to anyone else, except abroad letting them know everything that had happened, to the U.N., Amnesty International etc., I always received a reply in which they told me that they had asked Pinochet for information but that they had not yet received a reply. My husband is German, in spite of the fact that he has lived in Chile for more than 40 years he never wanted to become naturalized and I never asked him to, because you don't become a citizen just by having a piece of paper, for this reason my son had the possibility to go to Germany if he wished, we went to the German Embassy to request a residency permit in Germany in case Jorge reappeared, they gave it to me saying that he could settle there when he was released, I think the embassy knew very well that my son was detained but they did nothing other than give me the permit. Or maybe they knew the fate of the Detained-Disappeared? That question has always stayed with me.

In 1976 Pinochet sent some information to the U.N. about the prisoners we had been asking for, it says in that information that 150 of the names who had been asked for as Detained had no legal existence that they were invented names, in that list was Jorge's name, in view of that we go to the Embassy to tell them of the monstrosity of that information, then the Embassy sends a letter to the Ministry of Foreign Affairs complaining about this, they receive a reply on paper with the letterhead of the Ministry of Foreign Affairs. Among their replies to the Embassy's questions they say "that by a regrettable error the name Jorge Muller was included on this list, that they were going to investigate" the signature of that letter was a scribble, nobody taking responsibility, nobody who could be identified the gutless bastards hiding their evil face, from the beginning.

The search for my son Jorge marked out a path for me that I never thought I would make. When I talked with my son I always told him I was very old to begin to do new things, at that time I wasn't yet 50 years old and thought that at that stage of life one should enjoy a certain tranquillity and just wait for grandchildren, then he told me mama how can you think that at this stage you are too old to do things look at don CLOTARIO BLEST labour leader all his life and at that time he was about 50 years old; it took the loss of my son for me to realize that for the struggle there is no age, even if it is true that a woman can't come out firing a gun but thank God she has a mind and ideas for doing things, things I have been doing all these years, I never could have stayed at home with my arms folded, the greatest homage I can render to my son is to take up his battle flag in a certain way I have done it, I am an active member of the Association of Families of the Detained-Disappeared, occupying also posts within the organization, I make arpilleras as a way of denouncing the problem by means of needlework, this I have been doing almost from the very moment of the disappearance of my son, in the Pro-Paz Committee they offered us guidance to make these arpilleras, they were always looking for forms to lessen the anguish we were living, there were also paintings on cloth, knitting, in other words as I said it was to appease the anguish for some, and for the others a little economic gain, many of our companions had had their husband or head of household Disappeared. Another of the activities that helped me to overcome the anguish has been the teaching of Chilean folklore, of which I had some knowledge because I enjoyed it but never practiced it, but in 1978 I worked in the East Zone where the Vicarate of Solidarity had assigned us because we lived in that zone. I made contact with unemployed workers, wives of unemployed men who also made arpilleras, with people from the poor neighbourhoods who always come to the regional offices of the Vicarate in search of solutions to so many problems. In other words, many people, then I thought, why not make my knowledge of folklore available to these people? There is so much need of a little relaxation to mitigate a little all the pain my own as well as that of those companions that I often saw almost fainting from hunger, I thought it might even be a little like a sacrilege to put on an activity as festive as singing and dancing with everything that's going on, but I myself gave myself courage I talked with a young man who is a very good musician so that he could take charge of the music and I of everything else, that's how we started this folklore group of songs and dances of Chiloé in August, 1978, by the month of September they were already asking us to present a program, and we have been going ever since, not just putting on performances but also offering instruction to groups of young people in the poor neighbourhoods, all this we have almost done by our own efforts this past year we had some support from a cooperating organization from abroad, which permitted us to buy instruments we needed, the group is united. They present their programs in the

112

children's feeding centres, in the shantytowns, to Unions on Strike, in other words, wherever our presence is necessary, with the only expense that they furnish us with transportation, the majority of the people who make up this group are unemployed, but the spirit of each one is totally committed. Doing this work I can say has served to keep me physically as well as morally strong to continue carrying on the fight to know what happened with the Detained-Disappeared.

The tasks of the Association are numerous, every day there is something to do, the spirits of all family members remain high, there is a unanimous consciousness that the search must continue and we are always searching for ways and more ways to keep the knowledge of our problem alive, for us the pressure that can be applied from abroad asking about our family members is of great importance. We women know that Pinochet regards us as old madwomen who are stirring up his little chicks, the man doesn't know the spirit of each one of my companions in spite of having been detained, in spite of having spent time in Jail as has happened with various women, recently a companion of the Association was released after being detained several months, the dictators think that all that will terrify us, they are mistaken up down and sideways, they assassinate people who are very closely allied with us in our continual battle, also to terrify us, and they don't realize that the indignation runs over seeing the hands in which our poor Country is.

I hold to a Christian faith for that reason I ask God to grant me life yet, because I believe I could not die in peace if I don't know what happened to my son. The years I have lived through weigh down like thousands of years, I wrote a few lines that say:

My hair has turned white
My eyes sad and tired
So many tears have been shed
In these past years
I live the question
Will I see him one day?
I wait anxiously
it must be so

The poem goes on, I have written a number of things, I never thought that pain could also be a source of inspiration, I only write popular verses, mine are folkloric verses that say everything very simply.

What I have done up to now I will continue doing in the same way because I think that is the only way I can survive, at times I am so tired and would like to do nothing, but then I reproach myself for such an attitude, I take a deep breath, throw my shoulders back and say to myself, Jorge expects you to continue doing what he could not do, and I will do it, I will do it.

Santiago de Chile   April, 1985

Testimony #7

Santiago August 22, 1983

Senora,

Dear remembered companion I hope you and your family are well, I am writing to have news of you. I have still not recovered from my arm and hand, only on August 17 they took off the cast, I had three fractures and still today my fingers hurt me a lot although by now I can pick up some things, I thought I wasn't going to recover the use of my hand, the time has seemed very long to me not being able to work. Dear friend, you know how we are living we Chileans, incredible that there is no respect for human life not even children, it is an atmosphere of uncertainty. The funerals of so many innocent people have been very moving, how we wished you could have been with us in these so difficult months we are going through and will continue to go through, but the day is not far off when we will see each other again, in our own free Country, and we won't be hiding as we were a few days ago, our family members of the suffering disappeared and we will go on with the painful drama, we go out in the street with the photos of our dear disappeared ones in difficult hours.

But it doesn't bother the government much, now the political situation is worse, they arrest people and beat them. The 10th of this month we went out and various of our companions were left with lesions on their arms and chests, now they don't respect us. Before they used to arrest us but they didn't beat us, we go out knowing that they are going to take away our photos rip them up and insult us and more than that we are not going to keep still without complaining. I went out with my arm and hand in a cast, my companions told me to stay in my house since I was injured . . .

My dear companion write to me You know that your letters encourage me I will tell you that my nerves are so bad that the psychologist is seeing me every 10 days, I suffered so much because of what we are living through . . .

Best greetings from me and from Claudio. Greetings to your husband and the girls and Monolito ask to be remembered.

Testimony #8

Santiago, January 14, 1985

My story is very simple and more than that sad, I belong to the Association of Families of Detained-Disappeared and am arpillerista at the same time, when I make the arpilleras I am thinking not only of my own problem, but of all the families without distinction because of political beliefs. This work is done under the wing of the Vicarate, that also buys the work from us, that helps us to survive. The work began ten years ago, with the object of denouncing to the world what was happening in Chile, regarding the disappearance of thousands of Chileans beginning from the 11th of September, 1973. The suffering and anguish for my daughter, daughter-in-law and little grandchildren and myself is very great, but still I don't lose hopes of seeing my son alive again. In addition our association has a folklore group and from time to time we have a get-together in the Association where in spite of the sadness, we enjoy ourselves and have a good time.

115

Well, there's a lot of tell but I don't find the words to tell it, in addition, here I enclose a short biography of my son not very complete, because there is a tremendous lot to tell about my beloved son. I beg you to denounce what has happened and to ask in the name of our family especially that my son Agustin A. Mártinez Meza, be returned alive from the tyranny of the dictator.

Through you we send greetings to all people interested in our problem and especially to You.

Affectionately, a mother.

Testimony #9

ACCOUNT OF THE DETENTION AND DISAPPEARANCE OF AGUSTIN A. MARTINEZ MEZA

He studied at the Industrial High School of San Miguel, finishing the course on December 30, 1966 and graduating as a Lathe Mechanic. Later he entered the U.T.E. (State Technical Univ.) graduating as a Mechanical Engineer on June 9, 1971. Beginning in 1971 he worked at the University of Chile as head of maintenance and professor of Technology. Later he left and began to work in the I.C.A., Ingenieros Consultores Asociados (Engineering Consultants Associates). In 1973 he was examiner of the applications for admission in Section No. 41, Santiago Liceo de Nombres No. 6.

Agustín, son, husband and father all at the same time, maintained two households, that of his widowed mother with a daughter, and his own. My son was deeply disturbed by the social problems, that for him were his own since he came from a modest home and from an early time had to assume responsibilities since his father died when he was barely nine years old.

AGUSTIN ALAMIRO MARTINEZ META.

Born in Santiago, March 26, 1947.

Identity card No. 105.806 - Office of La Serena.

Married 2 children; Christián and Fabián

Mechanical Engineer

PROCEDURES

Case No. 13920-2. 9th Criminal Court of Major Offenses of Santiago.
Case No. 13920-2. The Court of Appeals of Santiago rejected the petition for the protection of civil rights presented in favour of the injured party on the 26th of March, 1975. On being informed by the required authorities, the Minister of Interior and others, that he had not been detained, the evidence was returned to the 9th Court where the case was originally heard. The negative report of the authorities carries extremely grave consequences, since there are eyewitnesses to the detention.

BRIEF DESCRIPTION OF THE EVENTS:

My son Agustín Martínez Meza was arrested the 10th of January, 1975 about 19 hours near the house of his sister-in-law Elsa Moralez M. where he happened to be passing by momentarily. At the time he was arrested by agents of D.I.N.A. — now C.N.I., his little son Christián who was only one-and-a-half years old was with him. The events were witnessed by my son's mother-in-law Elsa Morales M., Carlos Páez, brother-in-law of the disappeared, Gloria Páez M., wife of the disappeared, Felicia Rodríguez M., sister, and by me, his mother, Emilia Meza.

In the hearing eyewitnesses to the detention testified, nevertheless the authorities continue to deny that the detention ever took place.

It was presented to the Court that the name of the injured party figured in the list of the 119 Chilean extremists who died abroad, faced with that information the Minister of Foreign Affairs said that the case under consideration and other cases (on the list) had never received any confirmation whatsoever.

As a result of the publication of these lists from abroad the President of the Military Junta requested a thorough investigation to establish the truth of the situation of the 119 persons, whose family members are demanding to know what has happened to them.

My son, Agustín A. Martínez Meza was born in the community of Nuñoa March 30th, 1947, he entered the school on Macul Street and Bellavista when he was six years old, at the age of 10 he was involved in Scout activities and the children's soccer team of the school. Then when he was 11 he became a boarding student at "Los niños cantones" (Cantonal Children) when the school was located on Pio Nono Street, near San Cristobal hill. When the priest don Fernando Larrain, headmaster and director of the school died, Agustín transferred to the Liceo Mirialdo and after the 2nd year of Humanities he entered the Industrial High School of San Miguel, located near the bus stop number twelve of Santa Rosa. There he was immediately awarded a scholarship by the Corfo (Corporación de Fomento, an agency charged with the development of roads) because of his interest in his studies and his good conduct observed both by his professors and by his school mates. He was always very cheerful and playful. Then he was elected president of the Alumni Centre of the School and was nominated to be the president of the Industrial Students, a post he did not accept, because he was in his last year getting a degree as lathe technician. In 1965 he entered the Masters' Program at Maestranza Jupiter, working as a Master Mechanic from December 20 to February, 1966.

After receiving his bachillerato in mathematics he entered the State Technical University, in la Serena in April, 1966 to study Mechanical Engineering. There he was the student director of the Student Centre representing the interests and wishes of the student body. During the 1970s, from January 6 to February 7, he received the practical training in his specialty by working for the Mine of Africa Company called "el Teniente." In 1971 Agustín Martínez Meza graduated from the U.T.E. (State Technical University) with the degree of Mechanical Engineer. In 1972 he worked as Mechanical Engineer of the University of Chile, as head of Maintenance and professor of Technology. He also worked as a projective draftsman in "El Teniente." Later he left the University of Chile for a job with a higher salary and started to work at I.C.A. (Consulting Engineers Associates) as head draftsman.

My first son was outstanding as a student and as a worker, was known among his companions for his selfless interests and aspirations for workers as a whole, seeing their differing skills and trades as the only difference between them. His actions were always guided by his loyal and humanitarian spirit in his dealings with his companions in school and later at work, with whom he shared not only the labours of the workplace, but in addition dedicated himself to serving and aiding his friends in poor neighbourhoods and surrounding marginal areas. Because of his interest in studying he obtained a scholarship and kept it for nine years, being the only student who had kept a fellowship for so many years.

In 1972 he married a University student, Señorita Gloria Páez.

There's a great deal to tell about Agustín, who was always a very good son, husband and brother, until he was detained and disappeared the 10th of January, 1975. Detained just in the New Year with all the gaiety the New Year signifies, but in Chile there was already much suffering. That day they arrested him in the street near his sister-in-law's house, with his little son only one-and-a-half year old, striking him in front of the baby, the child was returned to his home, by his father and the two individuals of D.I.N.A. now C.N.I. — This event caused the child serious psychological disorders. One day when little Christián was travelling on the bus with his mama, a cop got on, Christián was so furious he went to where the cop was sitting and hit him, saying you took my papito away, the guy got off the bus immediately.

Nowadays, my solitude and anguish is very great, at not having any news of my beloved son. I will never lose hope of having my son at my side again and holding him close in my arms.

Agustín, today and forever you will be present in our hearts.

Recounted by his mother.

Testimony #10

BIOGRAPHY OF ISIDRO MIGUEL ANGEL PIZARRO MENICONI
DETAINED AND DISAPPEARED IN CHILE

—UNDER ORDERS FROM THE ADMINISTRATION OF NATIONAL INTELLIGENCE D.I.N.A.

Isid o Pizarro Meniconi was born December 8, 1952, his childhood was spent surrounded by various brothers and sisters, since he was the fifth of thirteen children, in a well-established home where mutual respect toward others was primary. Isidro even then was clearly an alert child, observant, intelligent, and very loving toward his brothers and sisters, to his friends in school and in the neighbourhood.

He attended a primary school, until he finished his basic studies. During the whole time, years, that he spent there he was outstanding for being the best student in his class.

Then he carried out his higher level studies in the industrial high school No. 2. There he specialized in I.B.M. typewriters.

Because of his spirit of comradeship and responsibility he was elected President of the Student Centre later managing to be student director of the Federation of Trade Students of Chile. In light of this responsibility and representing the interests and demands of the student body he participated in such Congresses as the one called Science and Technology.

Since we come from a modest background, he understood while still a young child the difference between social classes and the effort a working man has to make in order to educate his children. An extremely valuable experience that he knew how to use to advantage in the battles in which he became involved to defend the interests of those most humble and exploited, the workers.

During his vacations he worked with farm labourers, those workers of the earth always left behind and shoved to one side when it comes to the advantages of life in the large cities, matters of education, technical instruction, health, etc. It is there in his contact with them that he began teaching them beginning with the real situation in which they lived, the value and dignity of man with regard to society.

Later he entered the University in 1973, specializing in subterranean water, but conscious of his political work and his commitment to the rights of workers, especially the peasants he didn't continue with his studies since they could wait or be postponed, in comparison with something that was much more urgent which was the fight for the rights and demands of the workers, one day the installation of a Popular Revolutionary Government might be accomplished, when the dignity of the working man and his family would be respected.

That's how he came at that time to be dedicated completely and entirely to the leadership and education of peasants, since they were in a totally abandoned and backward state. In the middle of this battle he was surprised by the 11th of September, 1973 because of this he was persecuted by the owners of tracts of land that the peasants, together with him, had managed to tear from the hands of the medium-sized and large plantation owners and parcel them out to those to whom they really belonged, that is, to the men who worked the earth, the peasants.

Then the 19th of November, 1974, he was detained, treated savagely by men from the Headquarters of National Intelligence, D.I.N.A. An organization dependent solely and exclusively upon the President of the Chilean Military Junta — Pinochet. On that cursed day they detained him putting him in the ill-fated position of a Political Detained-Disappeared. He had just turned 22 years of age, a life physically cut off leaving his companion and their two children to await him with the hope of being able to embrace him and get to know him again some day. But we should say that ramifications of his work still continue among many workers that keep on with dedication, courage and conscience this fight that history has given them.

ISIDRO MIGUEL ANGEL PIZARRO MENICONI
— YOU LIVE AND ARE IN EVERY WORKER
OF THIS CHILE
— PRESENT NOW AND FOREVER.
YOUR FIGHT WAS NOT IN VAIN. IT HAS GROWN
BRANCHES AMONG THE WORKING CLASS
AND   THE   PEOPLE   REMEMBER

YOU FOR YOUR EXAMPLE.

YOUR MOTHER

Santiago, July, 1977

I throw this letter to the wind so that it might carry the echo of my voice wherever you may be so you may know that I carry you like a sleeping dove in the hearts of children or a white rose cultivated in the hearts of mothers.

You are in the prayers of those persecuted, in the hopeful look of the oppressed, you are in the path of those sacrificed in the country of the exiles.

In the banner that burns in the air of Liberty.

You are in the redeeming star of those who sing, in the collective song of the people, in the permanent ideal of humanity.

You are in the life that God spreads over the earth.

Therefore I beg you and wish you to be strong so I also can see it and let the leaves of the calendar keep falling I hope that in some turn of the road we will meet one another.

This is my Christmas wish for you.

XII 80   (December 1980)

Testimony #11

QUESTION

Where is the son that I love so much?
Where is the warmth of his white hands?
When I call only silence responds.
Iron chains have left him prisoner,
and if you search blindly for your star in the night
you will only find shadows, sadness and reproaches.
What guard guards the bars of the dark cell that hides you?
they have left me a wound that is uncertainty
and I shout your name that the wind carries away,
my throat is raw from calling you.

But in your absence there is no forgetting
Yes, I lost the laugh that ripped the autumn
Summers wander in my sea of bitterness
winter goes with me with its sadness
and I let the impalpable rain kiss my forehead
asking God for the hand that wounds me with nostalgia
and I go on living from sips of the pain of knowing you absent
invisible is the dagger piercing my soul
and my face carries wounds caused by weeping
the slow step of the years, and grief beneath the song.
9 Dec., 1982

Testimony #12

NAME   : PIZARRO MENICONI,
                  ISIDRO MIGUEL ANGEL
I.D. NUMBER   : 62.233.627 (Passport)
CIVIL STATUS   : Bachelor
DATE OF BIRTH   : December 8, 1962
AGE   : 22 years
HOME ADDRESS   : Joaguín Godoy 315, La Reina
PROFESSION   : Typewriter mechanic
POSITIONS HELD : Director of peasant movement (regional).
                  Activist MIR (Movimiento Internacional
                  Revolucionary/International Revolutionary
                  Movement).

EVENTS

The 19th of November, 1974 Isidro M. Angel Pizarro Meniconi
arrived at his house in a vehicle of white colour, year 70, license
plate JV 587 of Providencia, accompanied by Ida Vera Almarza. As
they entered the house at 17 hours they were met by a hail of bullets,
since agents of D.I.N.A. were waiting for them inside the house.
    Isidro M. Angel Pizarro as well as the young woman Vera

Almarza fell wounded by the bullets.

The night of the day of the detention the house of the mother of Isidro Pizarro was searched by four agents of D.I.N.A. who carried firearms.

One of the individuals was carrying in his hand the identity card of Isidro Pizarro; when the mother asked various times what had happened to her son, they answered that "they wanted to know what her son had to do with what happened a few days ago."

Hours later Hipólito Pizarro arrived at his mother's house to tell her that his brother had fallen wounded by men in the Security.

The 25th of July, 1975 Isidro M.A. Pizarro was mentioned in a list as dead in a confrontation abroad.

Between the days 25th of November of 1974 and the 18th of December, 1975 he was seen in Auilín (red light district), Villa Grimaldi, the Santa Lucía Clinic, all places under the charge of D.I.N.A.

The complaint issued by the mother Doris Meniconi Lorca, housewife, living at Cochamó 1431, of Conchalí, Santiago, identity card No. 4.884.779-K, of Santiago, in the 11th court of Major Offenses, relates the events thus: "During the year 1974 my son rented from don Jorge Guillermo Darhmen Alcaíno an apartment in the interior of the property located in Joaquín Godoy No. 315 of La Reina, together with the architect doña Ida Vera Almarza and various other friends. The 19th of November of the aforementioned year my son arrived at his domicile around 17 hours, accompanied by Miss Vera and another friend, travelling in an automobile Dodge Dart Model 1970, white, license plate JV 587 from Providencia.

A little before he arrived, there had arrived at his domicile various men of the armed security forces, who had searched the interior apartment that he occupied with no warrant whatsoever. When the landlord Jorge Darhman arrived, he was detained by the agents, who questioned him about the occupants of the apartment. The agents obliged him to stay with them while they waited for the arrival of his tenants. When my son arrived a violent outburst of shooting took place, as a consequence of which Ida Vera as well as I. Pizarro were wounded and detained. At that hour my son Hípólito

Pizarro Meniconi neared the place, for the purpose of visiting his brother. From a short distance away he witnessed these events and could see how Isidro was shot in the legs by the agents after he had already been detained. On hearing what had happened agents from the 23rd Commissary of Carabineros appeared at the scene. On meeting the agents, they identified themselves as belonging to the Headquarters of the National Intelligence, D.I.N.A., at which the Carabineros withdrew, without interfering in anything more. They could see, however, into the interior of the house the two detainées, both wounded. Among the officers of the Carabineros who came to the scene is the permanent officer of the 23rd Commissary, lieutenant Hugo Urrutia González, the deputy commissioner, Major Domingo Zabaleta and one of the heads of the Oriente Prefecture, Lieutenant Colonel Omar Torrecilla.

"At dusk of that day, and before I had heard about what had happened, being at home with my husband, Isidro Pizarro Andaluce, four men in civilian clothes arrived, showing an identify card of which I was only able to read the phrase "Intelligence Service." They asked for my son Isidro, and then proceeded to search the entire house, without showing any legal warrant for it. They took nothing, I kept insisting to them that my son didn't live with us, but they remained silent."

Later she added: "The shooting and the detentions were commented on at great length next day in the press, without the names of those detained being given. Express mention was made of the fact that agents of D.I.N.A. had carried out the operation.

"Then, total silence. My son was never put at the disposition of a proper tribunal, neither convicted nor set free."

Commenting in more detail regarding the presence of the Intelligence Service in her house the night of the day the detention took place, the mother of the detainée tells what happened in the course of her statement entered as part of the Petition for the Protection of Civil Rights, Rol. 1.588-74 of the date 16th of December, 1974: "On the 19th day of November, 1974 four men in civilian clothes came to my house without identifying themselves with identification papers but verbally they said they belonged to the

125

Service of Military Intelligence; when my husband asked the reasons for this impestuous visit, they responded that "it's none of your business;" they carried the identification card of my son Isidro Pizarro Meniconi, single, 22 years old, working as a typewriter repair man, they indicated they wanted to "know his connection with an event of a few days ago." They said no more, but my son was never seen again, and the fact that they were carrying his identification card confirms to me the fact of his detention.

"The men in civilian clothes were driving a red van with a black top, license plate XX 598."

As confirmation of these facts, there exists the sworn statement of the brother of the detainée, an eyewitness to the events, in addition to the declarations made in the hearing for the disappearance of Ida Vera, Rol. 1.302-9 of the 11th Court of Major Offenses of Santiago (Separate file). The testimony of Guillermo Darhmen Alcaíno, who had rented the apartment in which the detainées lived, and who was detained in his own house by men in civilian clothes who searched it and stayed there awaiting the arrival of Ida and Isidro: This is the eyewitness account of the events. Also the statements of the Lieutenant of Carabineros Hugo Guillermo Urrutia González, who admits specifically the action of D.I.N.A. and that there were two persons wounded — a man and a woman — and that he saw when they were carried away by personnel from D.I.N.A. In addition, the statements of the Major of the Carabineros Domingo Zabaleta Mendoza, who admits having been positioned in the street of J. Godoy 315, on being informed that there had been a shooting among civilians, confirming that the procedure had been carried out by personnel of D.I.N.A.

In addition to verification of the events of the detention by the witnesses already mentioned, other evidence exists that indicates that the detainée was in the hands of D.I.N.A. at a date later than the detention. There are even testimonies about his physical condition.

The mother of the detainée declared in the complaint of the 11th Court of Santiago: "In December of 1974 I was informed in the offices of the International Red Cross that the detainée had been visited by personnel of that organization in Villa Grimaldi. I never received any further information either then or later.

"In the Petition for Protection of Civil Rights presented for Isidro, Rol. 1.388-74, the authorities informed the court that the detainée was to be interned in the Military Hospital. After learning that information I went to that hospital establishment. An employee told me my son was not there, but, with undoubted knowledge of the case, added that "he had police protection and medical assistance wherever he was." As incredible as it may seem he added, "Your son is worth more alive." Neither was it possible for me to obtain any other information in the Military Hospital in the future."

Later she declared: "to give even more credibility to the events described, both Ida Vera as well as Isidro Pizarro were seen after their detention in secret locations branches belonging to D.I.N.A., both in Villa Grimaldi, and in a house located in Auilín Street, the Macul section, known as the "venda sexy," sexy strip, or red light district. Ida informed other women prisoners in great detail about her detention and that of Isidro, how they were carried for treatment of their wounds to a clinic, located at 162 Santa Lucía Street, and later returned to the place where they were all together. Their names are: Cristina Verónica Godoy Hinojosa, Bernadita Núñez Rivera and Beatriz Bataszow Contreras. Their declarations that appear in the evidence in the hearing for the disappearance of Ida Vera, Rol. 1.302-9, which was transacted before this court, should be available to be seen and are overwhelming in the details they give of that place of detention and the state in which the detainée (Ida) was found at the time of her conversations with them."

There also exists a written statement sent from Costa Rica by Ana María Romero, dated February 22, 1976, in which she declares she was held with Ida Vera Almarza in the same location where Isidro Pizarro was also held. Ida Vera told her what had happened to her and to Isidro Pizarro, as well as the tortures to which they were subjected. She affirms that she knew from other detainées that on December 24th at dawn a group of detainées were taken out including Ida and Isidro. Since that moment nothing more has been known of them.

In July of 1974 the daily newspaper O DIA of Curitiba, Brazil, published a list of 59 Chilean citizens supposedly killed in a confrontation with regular troops of the Argentinian army in the province of Salta. This list included the name of Isidro Pizarro Meniconi, information that received wide publicity by all the Chilean media (case of the "119").

The Chilean Government informed the Interamerican Commission of Human Rights of the OAS (Organization of American States) that: "The Federal Argentinian police has manifested that it is not conceivable that an event of such magnitude could have occurred in the Republic (of Argentina) without the knowledge of the proper authorities."

The scandal of the case of the "119" was never clarified and Isidro Pizarro Meniconi is still missing.

LEGAL ACTIONS

A Petition for the Protection of Civil Rights Rol. 1.588-74, was filed the 16th day of December of 1974, was rejected the 7th day of April, 1975. The decision was appealed to the Supreme Court which upheld the original finding on the date of 14th of April of 1975.

Criminal complaint filed in the month of November of 1977, in the 11th Court of Major Offenses of Santiago, for the crimes of kidnapping, grave injury, and prolonged status of incommunicado.

Non-Judicial testimony

The father of the injured party, Isidro Humberto Pizarro A., was detained the 15th of September of 1973 after a search of Pasaje Cochamó 1431, La Palmilla, his house, with the purpose of determining the whereabouts of his son. That is, according to the military statement the injured party was being sought by security organizations.

The 24th of December of the same year, the house of the parents of the injured party was again searched, for the same stated purpose.

The 4th of June 1974 the house of the older brother of the injured party, located in Arturo Prat Street 1952, was searched and the brother was detained and indicted.

Testimony #13

NARRATIVE

My son Gerardo Ernesto Silva Saldivar, technical student in statistics at the University of Chile, 23 years old, Chilean identity card #6222736 of Santiago. Detained the 10th day of December of 1974 about 12:30 o'clock of that day, by agents of D.I.N.A. as he exited the University Library, where he had been preparing for final exams. Those arresting him were driving a late model green van, they did not identify themselves or show any kind of arrest warrant, armed with machine guns, they proceeded to search my son in plain view on the street, keeping him covered the whole time with their guns. All of this was observed by numerous passers-by who were going along the street, the location being the intersection of the streets of San Martín and Augustinas, the place of the detention.

That same day around 2 o'clock in the morning, an operation was carried out by 8 heavily armed individuals apparently composed of the same group that detained my son, our domicile was searched without any identification or any kind of legal order being shown that would authorize such a search. My son was not in our house, since for the past two years he had not lived in the family household. The numerous efforts to locate him were fruitless and they violated our individual rights in the process. My husband and I filed a Petition for the Protection of Civil Rights in favour of our son, rol 1617-74 which was not accepted by the higher courts of justice of my country. I made a complaint for false arrest, rol 23667-2 in the 3rd Criminal Court of San Miguel, which was dismissed for lack of evidence, according to the Court. Later a request was made that the case be re-opened and new evidence was added to the case, causing it to become then a charge of kidnapping before the same Criminal

Court, rol 84227-5, with no positive results up to this day. Then after more than two years of incessant and the most diverse procedures and inquiries, feeling myself physically exhausted and terribly wounded in my moral and spiritual being, and all without having managed to have even a part of the situation regarding my son clarified or explained.

I should add that on the 23rd day of July of 1975 the Chilean press reported that 199 (this is referring to the case of the "119") Chilean "extremists" had died in the Republic of Argentina, the name of my son appeared in the list of names. Before such an unusual and incredible event, during which they tried to make my son reappear in Argentina, after he had been detained in Chile by agents of D.I.N.A., I made innumerable inquiries with the aim of clarifying the situation and from the investigations carried out in Argentina it was proved that the statement printed in the Chilean Press was totally false.

On the 20th of August of 1975 in the city of San Bernardo, President Pinochet announced that the government would make a wide investigation of the events but as of this date we have no reply that tells us the truth, that would end this uncertainty that is slowly killing us day by day.

Testimony #14

BIOGRAPHY

GERARDO ERNESTO SILVA SALDIVAR: born the 12th of May, 1951 in Santiago, from a small child was intelligent, at not quite 5 years of age he entered Public School No. 31 where he studied till the fourth preparatory year always being among the top of his class. The teacher predicted a bright future for him because of the ease with which he learned he never needed to review his lessons.

Then because we moved he continued his studies in Public School No. 346 of Sector A of the Población José María Caro, studied until the sixth preparatory year and in 1962 entered the first year of Business in the Institute of Applied Business on Eighteenth Street No. 216 of Santiago.

His personality already evident continued to develop day by day, open, affectionate and always ready to help others in whatever it might be, cheerful and always joking, with a great sense of humour, everyone who knows him loves him for the way he is. In the neighbourhood club to which he belonged he was always noted for his correct behaviour on the playing field.

He finished at the Institute in 1969, applied to the University of Economics and Technical Statistics and was accepted for both courses. Economics was taught in Arica and Statistics in Santiago, he really wanted to continue with Economics but our means did not reach far enough to cover the costs of his stay in Arica. Understanding this he entered the University of Chile in 1970 in the course of Technical Statistics. Before that he did his practical work as Accountant in the General Comptroller's Office of the Republic Company, the Andina Company and Port Company of Valparaíso.

While he was studying at the University he worked in Accounting at the Greco Shoe Company, took classes in mathematics and was the delegate of our block to the Neighbourhood Governing Body together with my husband, working for the good of the community, Población leader, exemplary son and brother, our family always united and tranquil lived happily. A tranquillity that ended with the cruel Military coup the 11th day of September, 1973 that brought with it pain and grief, since our Household had already been hit by the detention of Sonia, our oldest daughter, a medical technician of the Central Emergency Room, where she had worked since 1968, she was detained in the National Stadium and kept in the House of Correction three months and ten days as a Political Prisoner. She was the one who helped economically with the studies of her brothers, among them Gerardo. The months of relative calm that followed her release culminated with the Detention and Arbitrary Kidnapping of Gerardo the 10th of December, 1974.

131

Testimony #15

IF YOU KNEW

I WOULD LIKE YOU TO KNOW SON
THAT YOUR NAME RUNS
THROUGH THE BEADS OF MY ROSARY
to think that they made you disappear
just after you reached your 22nd year
If you knew son
how I search for you from dawn to dusk,
I know that your ideal was just
for your people, now their rights
are trampled on.

No longer are you with your people
but I will take your place
because I am sure that one day
our people will be freed.

There are companions prisoners fallen exiles
But those of us who remain will keep fighting
among young voices, fiery speeches
firm steps, ardent hearts, but always advancing.
United in this long fight like brothers
trusting in God with faith in His justice
because the whole world hears
the pain and prayers of so many mothers
Here I am, and here I stay,
in spite of the repression, but without fear
waiting for the return of those I don't have
to obtain justice and truth
a right of all the people
a right called *LIBERTY*.
May, 1982

Testimony #16

TO MY SONS, IN EXILE

The echo of your voices come to me
they are calling me
painful knowing they are alone
not being able to accompany them
painful knowing them sad, without being able to console them
I only ask that they understand
the purpose of my intense battle
which is that hope will bring them back
so I can embrace them.
September, 1976

Testimony #17

FOR YOU

If you don't return I won't stay here waiting for you
I will wander the roads in search of you
to find you in every companion
that carries your banner through the world
If you don't return I won't stop looking for you
I will find you on the road.

Bibliography

General Books on Contemporary Chilean Politics

Alaluf, David, et al. *Reforma Agraria Chilena: seis ensayos de interpretacion.* (Santiago: ICIRA, 1970).

Alexander, Robert J. *The Tragedy of Chile.* (Connecticut: Greenwood Press, 1978)

Alfonso, A., E. Klein, P. Ramírez, S. Gómez. *Movimiento campesino chileno.* (Santiago: ICIRA, 1970).

Algunos fundamentos de la intervención militar en Chile, Septiembre 1973. (Santiago: Editora Nacional Gabriela Mistral Ltda., 1974).

Altamiro, Carlos. *Decisión revolucionaria* (Santiago: Quimantú, 1973).

Angell, A. *Politics and the Labour Movement in Chile.* (London: Oxford University Press, 1972).

Arriagada, Genaro. *De la "via chilena" a la "via insurreccional".* (Santiago: Pacifico, 1974).

Arroyo, Gonzalo. *Coup d'etat au Chili.* (Paris: Editions du Cerf, 1974).

Baklanoff, Eric. *Expropiation of U.S. Investments in Cuba, Mexico and Chile.* (New York: Praeger Publishers, 1975).

Bello, Wladen F. *The Roots and Dynamics of Revolution and Counterrevolution in Chile.* Ph.D. Dissertation, Princeton University, 1975.

Subversion in Chile: a case study of U.S. Corporate Intrigue in the Third World. Bertrand Russell Peace Foundation, Nottingham, Eng., 1972.

Birns, Lawrence (ed.). *Chile and Allende.* (New York: Facts on File, 1974).

Birns, Lawrence. (ed.). *The End of Chilean Democracy: An IDOC Dossier on the Coup and its Aftermath.* (New York: Seabury Press, 1974).

Blanco, Hugo. *The Coup in Chile: Firsthand Report and Assessment.* (New York: Pathfinder Press, 1973).

Boizard, Ricardo. *El último día de Allende.* (Santiago, Chile: Editorial del Pacífico, 1973).

Bonilla, Frank and Myron Glazer. *Student Politics in Chile.* (New York: Basic Books, 1970).

Boorstein, Edward. *Allende's Chile: An Inside View.* (New York: International Publishing, 1977).

Brotherson, Victor. (editor). *Chile hoy.* (México: Siglo XXI, 1971).

Cademártori, José. *La economia chilena: un enfoque marxista.* (Santiago: Editorial Universitaria, 1968).

Camejo, Peter. *Allende's Chile, Is it Going Socialist?* (New York: Pathfinder Press, 1971).

Canihuante, Gustavo. *La revolución chilena.* (Santiago: Nascimento, 1971).

Caputo, Orlando and Roberto Pizarro. *Desarollo y capital extranjero: las nuevas formas del imperialismo en Chile.* (Santiago: Imp. Horizonte, 1970).

Casanueva, Fernando and Manuel Fernandez Canque. *El Partido Socialista y la Lucha de Clases.* (Santiago: Editorial Quimantú, 1973).

Castillo V., Jaime. *Las fuentes de la Democracia Cristiana. (Santiago: Editorial del Pacífico, 1963).*

Castro, Fidel and Beatriz Allende. Homenaje a Salvador Allende. (Buenos Aires: Editorial Galerna, 1973).

Castro, Fidel; Beatriz Allende and Raúl Roa. *Allende: combatiente y soldado de la revolución.* (Lima: Editorial Causachun, 1973).

IDOC. *Chile Under Military Rule (IDOC/North America, 1974).*

Cerda, Carlos. *Genocide au Chili.* (Paris: Francios Maspero, 1974).

Chilcote, Ron and Terry Dietz-Fee. "Assessing the Literature since the Coup", *Latin American Perspectives,* 1, Summer 1974; special issue: *Chile: Blood on the Peaceful Road).*

Chonchol, Jaques and Julio Silva. *El desarrollo de la nueva sociedad en America Latina.* (Santiago: Editorial Universitaria, 1969).

Cleaves, Peter S. *Bureaucratic Politics and Administration in Chile.* (Berkeley: Univ. of Calif Press, 1974).

Daugherty, Charles H. *Chile: Election Factbook.* (Washington: Institute for the Comparative Study of Political Systems, 1964).

De Vylder, Stefan. *Allende's Chile: The Political Economy of the Rise and Fall of the Unidad Popular.* (Cambridge: Cambridge University Press, 1974).

Debray, Régis. *The Chilean Revolution: Conversations with Allende.* (New York: Random House, 1971).

Díaz, Pablo (et al). *Chile: Una tragedia americana.* (Buenos Aires: Ediciones de Crisis, 1974).

Elqueta, Bernardo, et al. *Five Years of Military Government in Chile (1973-1978).* (Pine Plains, New York: Coleman 1980).

Evans, Les, ed. *Disaster in Chile: Allende's Strategy and Why it Failed.* (New York: Pathfinder Press, 1974).

Fidel In Chile: A Symbolic Meeting Between Two Historical Processes. (New York: International Publishers, 1972).

Faletto, Ruiz and Zemelman. *Génesis histórico del proceso politico chileno.* (Santiago: Quimantú, 1971).

Feinberg, Richard E. *The Triumph of Allende: Chile's Legal Revolution.* (New York: Mentor Books, 1972).

Foley, Gerry and Malik Miah. *Tragedy in Chile: Lessons of the Revolutionary Upsurge and its Defeat.* (New York: Pathfinder Press, 1973).

Foxley, Alejandro et al. *Chile: Búsqueda de un Nuevo Socialismo.* (Santiago: Ediciones Nueva Universidad, 1971).

Francis, Michael J. *The Allende Victory: An Analysis of the 1970 Chilean Presidential Election.* (Tuscon: Univ. of Arizona Press, 1973).

Frank, André. *Capitalism and Underdevelopment in Latin America: Historical Studies of Chile and Brazil.* (New York: Monthly Review Press, 1967).

Frei, Eduardo. *Pensamiento y acción.* (Santiago: Editorial del Pacífico, 1958).

Garcés, Joan E. *El estado y los problemas tacticos en el gobierno de Allende.* (Mexico: Siglo XXI, 1973).

Garcés, Joan E. *Allende y la experiencia chilena* (Barcelona: Editorial Ariel, 1975).

Garcés, Joan. *El pensamiento económico del gobierno de Allende* (Santiago: Editorial Universitaria, 1971).

Garcés, Joan. *Revolución, congreso y constitucion: el caso Toha.* (Santiago: Quimantú, 1972).

Garcés, Joan. *Salvador Allende: su pensamiento político.* (Santiago: Quimantú, 1973).

Gil, Federico G., Ricardo lagos E., and Henry A. Landsberger (eds.). *Chile at the Turning Point: Lessons of the Socialist Years, 1970-1973.* (Trans. John S. Gitlitz) (Philidelphia: Institute for the Study of Human Issues, 1979).

Halperin, Ernst. *Nationalism and Communism in Chile* (Cambridge, Ma: MIT Press, 1965).

Handelman, Howard and Thomas G. Sanders (eds.). *Military Government and the Movement Toward Democracy in South America.* (Bloomington: Univ. of Indiana Press, 1981).

Henfrey, Colin and Bernardo Sorj. *Chilean Voices.* (New Jersey: Humanities Press Inc., 1977).

Horowitz, Irving Luis. *The Rise and Fall of Project Camelot.* (Cambridge: MIT Press, 1967).

IDOC, *Chile: The Allende Years, The Coup, Under the Junta.* IDOC, no. 58, December 1973.

IDOC, *Chile Under Military Rule.* (New York: IDOC, 1974).

Jobet, J.C. and A. Chelen. *Pensamiento teorico y politico del Partido Socialista de Chile.* (Santiago: Quimantú, 1972).

Jobet, Julio César. *El Partido Socialista de Chile.* (Santiago: Ediciones Prensa Lationamerica, 1971) 2 vols.

Johnson, Dale. (ed.) *The Chilean Road to Socialism.* (New York: Anchor Books, 1973).

Joxe, Alain. *Las Fuerzas Armadas y el sistema político de Chile.* (Santiago: Editorial Universitaria, 1970).

Kaufman, Robert R. *The Politics of Land Reform in Chile 1950-1970.* (Cambridge, Ma.: Harvard University Press, 1972).

Kinsbruner, Jay. *Chile: An Historical Interpretation* (Cross-Currents in Latin America Series) (New York: Harper and Row, 1973).

Labarca Godard, Eduardo. *Chile al rojo* Santiago: Unversidad Técnica del Estado, 1971).

Latin American Bureau. *Chile: The Pinochet Decade.* (London: Latin American Bureau, 1983).

Lechner, Norbert. *La democracia en Chile.* (Buenos Aires: Ediciones Signos, 1970).

Loveman, Brian. *Chile: The Legacy of Hispanic Capitalism.* (London: Oxford University Press, 1979).

Loveman, Brian. *Struggle in the Countryside: Politics and Rural Labor in Chile, 1919-1973.* (Bloomington: Indiana Univ. Press, 1976).

MacEoin, Gary. *No Peaceful Way: The Chilean Struggle for Dignity* (New York: Sheed and Ward Press, 1974).

Mans, P. *La rebelion de la Escuadra.* (Valparaíso: Ediciones Nueva Universidad, 1973).

MAPU. *El segundo año de la revolución popular.* (Santiago: Editorial Unidad Proletaria, 1972).

Martner, G. *El pensamiento ecońomico del gobierno de Allende.* (Santiago: Editorial Universitaria, 1971).

Mattelart, Armand, Carmen Castillo and Leonardo Castillo. *La ideologia de la dominacion en una sociedad dependiente.* (Buenos Aires: Ediciones Signos, 1970).

Medhurst, Kenneth. *We Must Make Haste - Slowly: The Process of Revolution in Chile.* (New York: Vintage Books, 1973).

Morán, Theodore H. *Multinational Corporations and the Politics of Dependence: Copper in Chile.* (Princeton: Princeton Univ. Press, 1974).

Morris, James O. Elites, *Intellectuals and Consensus: A Study of the Social Question and the Industrial Relations System in Chile.* (Ithaca: Cornell Univ. Press, 1966).

NICH. *Subversion in Chile: The Complete Set of IT&T Memos,* Non-Intervention in Chile, Madison Wisconsin, n.d.

North American Congress on Latin America (NACLA). *New Chile* (New York: NACLA, 1972).

Novoa, Eduardo. *La batalla por el cobre.* (Santiago: Quimantu, 1972).

Nunn, Frederick M. *The Military in Chilean History: 1810-1973.* (Albuquerque: Univ. of New Mexico Press, 1976).

O'Brien, P., J. Roddick and I. Roxborough. *Chile: The State and Revolution* (London: Macmillan, 1975).

O'Brien, Philip J. (editor). *Allende's Chile.* (New York: Praeger Publishers, 1976).

Orrego, Claudio. *El paro nacional.* (Santiago: Editorial de Pacífico, 1972).

Palacios, Jorge. *Chile: An Attempt at "Historic Compromise", The Real Story of the Allende Years.* (Chicago: Banner Press, 1979).

Pastrana, Ernesto and Mónica Threlfall. *Pan, techo y poder: El movimiento de pobladores en Chile 1970-1973. (Buenos Aires: Ediciones S.A.P., 1974).*

Payró Lía, et al. Chile: Cambio de gobierno o toma de poder? (Mexico City: Editorial Extemporaneos, 1971).

Perlo, Victor. *End Fascist Terror and U.S. Imperialism in Chile.* (New York: New Outlook Publishers, 1974).

Petras, James and Hugo Zemelman Mirino. *Peasants in Revolt: A Chilean Case Study, 1965-1971.* trans. Thomas Flory. (Austin Univ. of Texas Press, 1972).

Petras, James and M.H. Morley. *How Allende Fell: A Study in U.S. – Chilean Relations.* (Nottingham, England: Spokesman Books, 1974).

Petras, James and Morris Morley. *The United States and Chile: Imperialism and the Overthrow of the Allende Government.* (New York: Monthly Review Press, 1974).

Petras, James. *Politics and Social Forces in Chilean Development.* (Berkeley: Univ. of Calif. Press, 1969).

Pío García, ed. *Las fuerzas armadas y el golpe de estado en Chile.* (Mexico: Siglo XXI, 1974).

Pike, F.B. *Chile and the United States 1880-1962.* (Notre Dame, Ind.: Univ. of Notre Dame Press, 1963).

Pike, Frederick B. *The Conflict Between Church and State in Latin America.* (New York: Alfred A. Knopf, 1925).

Ramirez Necochea, H. *Historia del imperialismo en Chile.* (Santiago: Editorial Austral, 1970).

Ramos, Sergio. *Chile: una economía de transicion?* (Santiago: Prensa Latinoamerica, 1972).

Rojas Sanford, Robinson. *The Murder of Allende and The End of The Chilean Way to Socialism.* (New York: Harper & Row, 1975).

Roxborough, Ian, Philip O'Brien and Jackie Roddick. *Chile: The State and Revolution.* (New York: Holmes & Meier Pub. Inc., 1977).

Sanders, Thomas G. *Chilean Self-Management Cooperatives During the Military Regime.* (American Universities Field Staff, Field Staff Reports, West Coast South America Series, No. 49.) (Hanover, New Hampshire: AUFS, December, 1979).

Sanders, Thomas G. *Military Government in Chile, Part I: The Coup.* (American Universities Field Staff, Field Staff Reports, West Coast South America Series, Vol. 22, No. 1) (Hanover, New

Hampshire: AUFS, December, 1975).

Sanders, Thomas G. *Military Government in Chile, Part II: The New Regime.* (American Universities Field Staff, Field Staff Reports, West Coast South America Series, Vol. 22, No. 2) (Hanover, New Hampshire: AUFS, December, 1975).

Shragin, Victor. *Chile: Corvalan Struggle.* (Moscow: Progress Publishers, 1980).

Sigmund, Paul E. *The Overthrow of Allende and the Politics of Chile: 1964-1976.* (Pittsburg: Univ. of Pittsburg Press, 1977).

Silva, Lautaro. *Allende: El fin de una aventura.* (Santiago: Ediciones Patria Nueva, 1974).

Smirnow, Gabriel. *The Revolution Disarmed: Chile 1970-1973.* (New York: Monthly Review Press, 1979).

Solar, Edmundo de. *Orlando Letelier.* (New York: Vantage, 1978).

Stallings, Barbara. *Class Conflict and Economic Development in Chile, 1958-1973.* (Stanford: Stanford University Press, 1978).

Steenland, Kyle. *Agrarian Reform Under Allende.* (Albuquerque: University of New Mexico Press, 1977).

Stephenson, John Reese. *The Chilean Popular Front.* (Philidelphia: Univ. of Pennsylvania Press, 1942).

Sweezy, Paul M. and Harry Magdoff, eds. *Revolution and Counter-Revolution in Chile.* (New York: Monthly Review Press, 1974).

Swift, Jeannine. *Agrarian Reform in Chile* (Lexington, Ma: D.C. Heath, 1971).

The I.T.T. Memos. Subversion in Chile: A Case Study of U.S. Corporate Intrigue in the Third World. (Nottingham, Eng.: Spokesman Books, 1972).

Thiesenhusen, William C. *Chile's Experiments in Agrarian Reform.* (Madison: Univ. of Wisconsin Press, 1966).

Touraine, Alain. *Vie et mort du Chile populaire.* (Paris: Seuil, 1974).

Valenzuela, Arturo and J. Samuel Valenzuela (eds.). *Military Rule in Chile: Neo-Liberalism and Dictatorship.* (Baltimore: Johns

Hopkins Univ. Press, 1982).

Valenzuela, Arturo and Samuel J. *Chile: Politics and Society.* (New Jersey: Transaction Books, 1976).

Valenzula, Arturo. *Chile: The Breakdown of Democratic Regimes.* (Baltimore: Johns Hopkins, 1978).

Varas, Florencia. *Coup.* (New York: Stein and Day, 1975).

Veneroni, Horacio L. *Estados Unidos y las fuerzas armadas de América Latina.* (Buenos Aires: Editorial Periferia, S.R.L., 1971).

Verdugo Marinkovic, Mario. *Esquema de los partidos y movimientos politicos chilenos y sintesis programatica de las candidaturas presidenciales en 1970.* (Santiago: Instituto de Ciencias Políticas y Administrativas, 1970).

continue April 8 on page 4.

Vidales, Carlos. *Contrarrevolución y dictadura en Chile.* (Bogota: Ediciones Tierra Americana, 1974).

Villanueva, Victor. *Modelo contrarevolucionario chileno.* (Lima: 1976).

Vuskovic, Pedro. *Acusación al imperialismo.* (Mexico City: Fondo de Cultura Económica, 1975).

Vylder, Stefan de. *Allende's Chile, The Political Economy of the Rise and Fall of the Unidad Popular.* (London: Cambridge Univ. Press, 1974).

Vylder, Stefan de. *Allende's Chile: The Political Economy of the Rise and Fall of the Unidad Popular.* (New York: Cambridge Univ. Press, 1976).

Whitaker, Arthur P. *The United States and the Southern Cone.* (Cambridge, Mass: Harvard University Press, 1976).

White Book of Change of Government in Chile September 11th 1973. (Empresa Editoria Nacional Gabriela Mistral Ltda., 1973).

Williams, Lee H (comp.). *The Allende Years.* (Boston: G.K. Hall, 1977).

Winn, Peter. *Weavers of Revolution. (New York: Oxford University Press, 1986).*

Wolpin, Miles D. Cuban Foreign Policy and Chilean Politics.

(Lexington: D.C. Heath, 1972).

Zammit, Ann. (ed.) *The Chilean Road to Socialism.* (Brighton, England: Institute of Development Studies at Sussex University, 1973).

Zeitlin, Maurice. *The Civil Wars in Chile (or the bourgeois revolutions that never were).* (Princeton: Princeton Univ. Press, 1984).

Articles

Alexander, Robert J. "Counterrevolution in Chile", *Current History*, 66, No. 389, Jan. 1974. p. 6-9.

Angell, Alan. "Chile After Five Years of Military Rule", *Current History*, 76, No. 448, Feb. 1979, 58-61, 88-89.

Angell, Alan. "Counter-revolution in Chile", *Current History*, *History*, 76, No. 448, February 1979, p. 58-61, 88-89.

Birns, Lawrence. "The Death of Chile", *The New York Review of Books*, XX, No. 17, November 1973.

Bizarro, Salvatore. "Rigidity and Restraint in Chile", *Current History*, 74, No. 436, ⌐ b. 1978, 66-69, 83.

Chile: "Blood on the F aceful Road". *Latin American Perspectives*, (Special Issue), 1, No. 2, Summer 1974.

García Márquez, Gabriel. "The Death of Salvador Allende", tr. Gregory Rabassa, *Harpers*, 248, no. 1486, March 1974, p. 53.

Gil, F.G. "Socialist Chile and the United States", *Inter American Economic Affairs*, vol. 27, Autumn 1973.

Hanson, S. "Kissinger on the Chilean Coup", *Inter American Economic Affairs*, vol. 27, Winter, 1973).

Hudson, Rexford A. "The Role of the Constitutional Conflict over the Nationalization in the Downfall of Salvador Allende", *Inter-American Economic Affairs*, 31, No. 4, Spring 1978, 63-79.

Johnson, Dale, John Pollack and Jane Sweeney. "ITT and the CIA: The Making of a Foreign Policy", *The Progressive*, May 1972.

Lagos, Ricardo and Oscar Rufatt. "Military Government and Real Wages in Chile". *LARR*, Summer 1975.

Lesser, Mishy and Steve Volk. "Ambush on the Peaceful Road", *Liberation*, XVIII, No. 3, November 1973.

Miliband, Ralph. "The Coup in Chile", *The Socialist Register 1973*, (London: Merlin, 1974).

Morley, Morris and Steven Smith. "Imperial Reach: U.S. Policy and the CIA in Chile", *Journal of Political and Military Sociology*, 5, No. 2, Fall 1977, 203-16.

NACLA. "Chile: The Story Behind the Coup", NACLA, *Latin America and Empire Report*, VII, No. 8, October 1973.

NACLA. "Liberated Documents: New Imperial Strategy for Latin America", NACLA's *Latin America and Empire Report*, VII, November 1971.

NACLA. "Secret Memos from ITT", NACLA's *Latin America and Empire Report*, VI, April 1972.

NACLA. Latin America and Empire Report: *Chile: Facing the Blockade*, (New York, 1973).

Nogee, Joseph L. and John W. Sloan. "Allende's Chile and the Soviet Union", *Journal of Inter-American Studies and World Affairs*, 21, No. 3, August 1979, 339-68.

North American Congress on Latin America. "The United States Propping Up the Junta", *Latin American and Empire Report*, Oct. 1974.

Petras, Betty and James. "Ballots into Bullets: Epitaph for a Peaceful Revolution", *Ramparts*, XII, No. 4, November 1973.

Petras, James. "Chile after Allende: A Tale of Two Coups", *Monthly Review*, XXV, No. 7, December 1973.

Petras, James. "The Transition to Socialism in Chile: Perspectives and Problems", *Monthly Review, 23, October 1971, pp. 43-71.*

Phillips, David A. *"Letter to Hortensia Bussi de Allende, 10 May 1975", Published in part in New York Times,* May 22, 1975, p. 37.

Plotke, David. "Coup in Chile" *Socialist Revolution,* No. 16, July-Aug. 1973.

Pollock, John, "Reporting on Chile: What the Press Leaves Out", The Nation (January, 19, 1973).

Sigmund, Paul E. "The Invisible Blocade and the Overthrow of Allende", *Foreign Affairs,* (January, 1974) p. 322-40.

Sweezy, Paul M. "Chile: The Question of Power", *Monthly Review,* XXV, No. 7, December 1973.

Valenzuela, Arturo and J. Samuel. "Visions of Chile", in *Latin American Research Review,* 10, Fall 1975.

Valenzuela, Arturo. "Eight Years of Military Rule in Chile", *Current History,* 81, No. 472, Feb. 1982, 64-68, 88.

Whitehead, Lawrence, "The Chilean Dictatorship", *World Today* (London), 32, No. 10, October 1976, 366-76.

Yglesias, José. "The Chilean Experiment: Revolution in the Countryside?", *Ramparts,* 11, June 1973, pp. 16-20.

Zeitlin, Maurice. "Chile: the Dilemmas of Democratic Socialism", *Working Papers,* I, No. 3, Fall, 1973.

Zimbalist, Andy and Barbara Stallings. "Showdown in Chile", *Monthly Review,* XXV, No. 5, October 1973. Jan. 1974.

Studies on Chilean and Latinamerican Women

Allende, Hortensia Bussi de. *Women and the Revolutionary Process in Chile.* (Los Angeles, California: Ediciones de la Frontera, 1972).

Allende, Isabel. "Lo que hace felíz a la mujer chilena en el amor", *Paula,* enero, 1971, pp. 65-70.

Andreas, Carol. *Nothing Is As It Should Be.* (Cambridge: Schenkman Pub. Co., 1976).

Boulding, Elise, Shirley A. Nuss, Dorothy Lee Carson and Michael A. Greenstein. *Handbook of International Data on Women.* (New York: Halsted Press, 1976).

Boulding, Elsie. *Women in the Twentieth Century World.* (New York: Sage, 1977).

Capezzuoli, L. and G. Cappabianca. *Historia de la emacipacion femenina.* (Buenos Aires: Editorial Futureo, 1966).

Carroll, Berenice A. (ed.). *Liberating Women's History.* (Urbana: Univ. of Illinois Press, 1976).

Chaney, Elsa M. "Old and New Feminists in Latin America: The Case of Peru and Chile" *Journal of Marriage and the Family,* 35, No. 2, May 1973, 331-43.

Chaney, Elsa. *Supermadre: Women in Politics in Latin America.* (Austin: University of Texas Press, 1979).

Chuchryx, Patricia Marie. *Protest, Politics and Personal Life: The Emergence of Feminism in a Military Dictatorship 1973-1983.* (Ph.D Dissertation, York University, Toronto, Ontario, 1986).

Duverger, Maurice. *The Political Role of Women.* (Paris: UNESCO, 1985).

Jaquette, Jane, ed. *Women in Politics* (New York: John Wiley and Sons, 1979).

Klimpel, Felicitas. *La mujer chilena: el aporte femenino al progreso de Chile.* (Santiago: Andrés Bello, 1963).

Kyle, Patricia A. and Michael J. Francis. "Women at the Polls: The Case of Chile, 1970-1971", *Comparitive Political Studies,* 11, No. 3, October 1978, 291-310.

Labarca Hubertson, Amanda. *Femenismo contemporaneo.* (Santiago: Zig-Zag, 1945).

Latin American and Caribbean Women's Collective. *Slaves of Slaves: The Challenge of Latin American Women.* Trans. Michael Pallis. (London: Zed Press, 1977).

Lavrin, Asunción. *Latin American Women: Historical Perspectives.* (Westport Connecticut: Greenwood Press, 1978).

Lindsay, J. *Comparative Perspectives on Third World Women* (New York: Praeger, 1980).

Mattelart, Michele. *La cultura de la opresion femenina.* (México: Ediciones Era, 1977). *Mujeres e industrias culturales.* (Barcelona: Cuadernos Anagrama, 1983).

Meller, Patricio. "Employment Stagnation in Chile: 1974-1978", *Latin American Research Review,* 16, No. 2, 1981, 144-55.

Miranda, Marta Elba. *Mujeres chilenas.* (Santiago: Editorial Nascimento, 1940).

Nash and Safa, ed. *Sex and Class in Latin America.* (Amherst: Bergin and Garvey Publishers Inc., 1980). *Women and Change in Latin America.* (Amherst: Bergin and Garvey Publishers Inc. 1984).

Partido Demócrata Cristiano. *Congreso Nacional de Mujeres Democratas Cristianas e Independientes: Congreso de la mujer chilena,* 23, 24 y 25 de Agosto, Valparíso, 1963 (Santiago: Imp. Sopech, 1963).

Paul, Catherine Manny. *Amanda Labarca H.: Educator to the Women of Chile.* (Cuernavaca: Centro Intercultural de Documentación, 1968).

Pereira, Teresa. *Tres ensayos sobre la mujer chilena.* (Valparaíso: Editorial Universitaria, 1978).

Paz, Amanda. *La mujer chilena.* (Santiago: Quimantú, 1972).

Remmer, Karen L. "Political Demobilization in Chile, 1973-1978", *Comparative Politics,* 12, No. 3, April 1980, 275-301.

Rowbotham, Sheila. *Women, Resistance & Revolution.* (New York: Vintage, 1974).

Salinas Bascur, Raquel. "Chilean Communications Under the Military Regime", *Current Research on Peace and Violence* (Tampere, Finland), No. 2, 1979, 80-85.

Santa Cruz, Adriana. *Comprolitan.* (Mexico: Editorial Nueva Imagen, 1980).

Sargent, Lydia (ed.). *Women and Revolution. (Boston: South End Press, 1981).*

Tinker, Irene, Michele Bo Bramsen and Magre Buvinic (eds.). *Women and World Development: With an Annotated Bibliography* (New York: Praeger, 1976).

U.N., Economic and Social Council, *Women and Education,* "Women and Education in Chile", by Amanda Labarca H. (Paris: UNESCO, 1953).

Veliz, Brunilda. "Women's Political Behavior in Chile". Master's Thesis, The Graduate School of the University of California at Berkeley, 1969).

Vitale, Luis. *Historia y sociologia de la mujer latinoamericana.* (Barcelona: Editorial Fontamara, 1981).

Church

Abbott, Walter M. (ed.). *The Documents of Vatican II.* (New York: America Press, 1966).

Bouvier, Virginia Marie. *Alliance of Compliance: Implications of the Chilean Experience for the Catholic Church in Latin America.*

Foreign and Comparative Studies, Latin American Series, No. 3. (Syracuse: Syracuse University, 1983).

Christians Concerned for Chile. "Chile after Four Years of Terror", *LUCHA: Christian Response to Military Repression in Latin America,* September 1977, pp. 2-35.

Gutierrez, Gustavo. *A Theology of Liberation.* (New York: Maryknolls, Orbis Books, 1973).

Kidnappings Lead to War of Words Between Church and Military", *Latin America Weekly Report* (London), WR80, No. 31, August 8, 1980, p. 7.

Lernoux, Penny. "The Latin American Church", *Latin American Research Review,* 15, No. 2, 1980, pp. 201-211.

Lernoux, Penny. *The Cry of the People: United States Involvement in the Rise of Fascism, Torture and Murder, and the Persecution of the Catholic Church in Latin America.* (New York: Doubleday, 1980).

Lernoux, Penny. "Suspensions of Chilean Students May Lead to Church-State Strife", *Chronicle of Higher Education,* 18, No. 20, July 23, 1979, pp. 5-6.

Mutchler, David E. *The Church as a Political Factor in Latin America: With Particular Reference to Colombia and Chile.* (New York: Praeger, 1971).

Sanders, Thomas G. *Popular Religion, Pastoral Renewal and National Reconciliation in Chilean Catholicism.* (American Universities Field Staff, Field Staff Reports, South America Series, No. 16) (Hanover, New Hampshire: AUFS, 1981).

Sanders, Thomas G. and Brian H. Smith. *The Chilean Church During the Allende and Pinochet Regimes,* American Universities Field Staff Reports, West Coast South America Series No. 23, March, 1976.

Sanders, Thomas G. and Brian H. Smith. *The Chilean Catholic Church During the Allende and Pinochet Regimes.* (American Universities Field Staff, Field Staff Reports, West Coast South America Series, Vol. 23, No. 1) (Hanover, New Hampshire: AUFS, March, 1976).

Sanders, Thomas G. Chile: *The "New Institutionality" and the "Consultation".* (American Universities Field Staff Reports. West Coast South America Series, No. 5) (Hanover New Hampshire: AUFS, 1978).

Sanders, Thomas G. *The Chilean Episcopate.* (American Universities Field Staff, Field Staff Reports, West Coast South America Series, Vo. 15, No. 3) (Hanover, New Hampshire: AUFS, August, 1968).

Smith, Brian H. "Christians and Marxists in Allende's Chile: Lessons for Western Europe", in *Religion and Politics in Western Europe,* Suzanne Berger, (London: Frank Cass, 1982).

Smith, Brian H. "Churches and Human Rights in Latin America: Recent Trends in the Subcontinent", *Journal of Interamerican Studies and World Affairs,* 21, February, 1979, pp. 89-128.

Smith, Brian H. "Human Rights in Latin American Political Culture: The Role of the Churches", p. 169-227 in Kenneth W. Thompson (ed.) *The Moral Imperatives of Human Rights: A World Survey.* (Washington: Univ. Press of America, 1980).

Smith, Brian H. "Old Allies, New Opponents: the Church and the Military in Chile, 1973-1979", (Paper presented and the workshop "Six Years of Military Rule in Chile" sponsored by Latin American Program, Woodrow Wilson International Center for Scholars, Smithsonian Institution) Washington: May 15-17, 1980.

Smith, Brian H. *The Church and Politics in Chile: Challenges to Modern Catholicism.* (Princeton: Princeton Univ. Press, 1982).

Vanderschueren, Franz and Jaime Rojas. "The Catholic Church of Chile: From 'Social Christianity' to Christians for Socialism'". *LARU Studies* 1 Feb. 1977, pp. 13-59.

Vicaria de la Solidaridad. un ano de labor. (Santiago: Arzobispado de Santiago, 1977). Also see 1978, 1979, 1980, 1981 (Internal Documents).

Human Rights
Documents and Testimonies

International Organizations
— Publications:

Banishment in Chile, Amnesty International Newsletter, (London), No. 8, August 1980, p. 4.

"Chile" pp. 53-55 in *Amnesty International Report 1979* (London: A.I. Publications 1979).

"Chile". pp. 122-128 in *Amnesty International Annual Report 1981.* (London: 1981).

Chile: An Amnesty International Report. (London: 1976).

Desapariciones. (Madrid: Editorial Fundamentos, 1983).

Desaparecidos: Disappeared in Chile, (Madrid: Editorial Fundamentos, n.d. 1977).

La tortura en Chile. (Madrid: Editorial Fundamentos, 1983). Trans. *(Chile: Evidence of Torture.)*

Prisioneros Desaparecidos en Chile. (Madrid: Editorial Fundamentos, 1979).

Torture in Chile. (London: 1974).

Torture in the Eighties. (London: A.I. 1984).

Testimonies and Articles

Anonymous. *Torture in Chile.* USLA Reporter, July-August, 1974.

Asociación Pro Derechos Humanos. "Chile: Balance de 10 años de dictadura", Editorial, *Derechos Humanos* (Madrid), verano 1983, p. 5.

Cancino Troncoso, Hugo. "La dictadura contra la sociedad", *Derechos Humanos*, verano 1983, p. 42.

Cayuela, José. *Chile. la masacre de un pueblo; testimonios de 9 Venozolanos victimas del golpe militar chileno.* (Caracas: Síntesis Dosmil, 1974).

Chile Committee for Human Rights. *Pinochet's Chile: An Eyewitness Report.* (London: Chile Committee for Human Rights, 1981).

Chile: State of War, *Eyewitness Report.* (Philidelphia: Woman's International League for Peace and Freedom, 1974).

Hauser, Thomas. *The Execution of Charles Horman: An American Sacrifice.* (New York: Harcourt Brace Jovanovich, 1978). (Hardcover, later published as *Missing*.)

La tragedia chilena: testimonios. (Buenos Aires: Merayo Editor, 1973).

Moffitt, Michael and Isabel Letelier. *Human Rights, Economic Aid and Private Banks: The Case of Chile.* (Washington: Institute for Policy Studies, 1978).

Munizaga, Giselle. *El discurso público de Pinochet* (Buenos Aires: Consejo Latinoamericano de Ciencias Sociales, 1983).

Pacheco G., Máximo. *Lonquén.* (Santiago: Editorial Anconcagua, 1980).

Report of the Chicago Commission of Inquiry into the Status of Human Rights in Chile (Chicago, 1974).

Soto Guzmán, Oscar. "Los derechos humanos en Chile", *Derechos Humanos,* verano 1983, p. 40.

The Moral Imperatives of Human Rights: A World Survey. (Washington: University Press of America, 1980).

Valdes, Hernan. *Tejas verdes: diario de un campo de concentracion en Chile.* (Barcelona: Editorial Ariel, 1974).

Villegas, Sergio. *Chile - El estadio: los crimenes de la junta militar.* (Buenos Aires: Cartago, 1974).

Marjorie Agosin's book is required reading for an understanding of the power and courage to be found in "scraps of cloth . . . scraps of life." Lives you won't forget. Through the burlap wall hangings known as arpilleras, artistry for women becomes a weapon of creative political action.

Geoff Hancock,
Canadian Fiction Magazine

SCRAPS OF LIFE is a pathbreaking work in women's history and in the study of the popular culture of resistance movements.

Temma Kaplan,
Barnard Women's Centre

A moving testimony to Chilean women's resistance to evil.

Joshua Rubenstein,
Amnesty Int'l., U.S.A.

Marjorie Agosin is from Chile and is a Professor of Spanish Literature at Wellesley College. She is the author of several books of poetry and her latest book is a critical work on Pablo Neruda. She lives in Boston with her husband, John Wiggins.